THE SIGNS *of a* PROPHET

The SIGNS *of a* PROPHET

THE PROPHETIC ACTIONS OF JESUS

MORNA D. HOOKER

TRINITY PRESS
INTERNATIONAL
HARRISBURG, PENNSYLVANIA

First U.S. edition published 1997
Trinity Press International
P.O. Box 1321
Harrisburg, PA 17105

Trinity Press International is division of The Morehouse Group.

First British edition published 1997 by SCM Press, London.

Library of Congress Cataloging-in-Publication Data

Hooker, Morna Dorothy
The signs of a prophet: the prophetic actions of Jesus/by Morna D. Hooker
p. cm.
"This book is an expanded version of the Schaffer lectures, delivered at Yale Divinity School in February 1995"—Pref.
Includes bibliographical references and index.
ISBN 1-56338-210-5 (alk. paper)
1. Jesus Christ—Prophetic office. 2. Prophets. I. Title.
BT252.H66 1997
232'.8—dc21   97-27070
                                                                        CIP

Cover painting by Robert Cariola

Printed in the United States of America

97 98 99 00 01 02   6 5 4 3 2 1

IN MEMORIAM

W. David Stacey

1923–1993

Contents

Preface

This book is an expanded version of the Shaffer lectures, delivered at Yale Divinity School in February 1995. I am grateful to the Dean and Faculty of the Divinity School for the invitation to give the lectures, and for their hospitality during my stay in New Haven. The lectures also formed the basis of the Smyth lectures, delivered at Columbia Theological Seminary, Decatur, in October 1996, and I am grateful to the Dean and Faculty of the Seminary for their invitation and hospitality.

I should also like to thank a number of friends for their comments on various parts of the typescript, among whom are Christopher Rowland, John Sweet, Robert Gordon and Anthony Bash.

The stimulus for the book came from my husband's work on *Prophetic Drama in the Old Testament* (Epworth Press 1990), which he intended as a prolegomenon to an investigation of the symbolism underlying the actions at the Last Supper. His ideas for this second volume were outlined in his Peake Memorial Lecture on 'The Last Supper as Prophetic Drama', given in June 1993. This was first published in the *Epworth Review*, Vol. 20, January 1994, and is included here as an appendix, by permission of the Methodist Publishing House. For the purposes of the Shaffer lectures, I decided to investigate the theme of Jesus' prophetic activity on a wider canvas, rather than concentrate solely on the Last Supper. This book is dedicated to David's memory, with love and gratitude for all he gave me.

Morna D. Hooker

Abbreviations

AGAJU	Arbeiten zur Geschichte des antiken Judentums und des Urchristentums
AJT	*American Journal of Theology*
Antt.	Josephus, *The Jewish Antiquities*
Apion	Josephus, *Contra Apionem*
BETL	Bibliotheca Ephemeridum Theologicarum Lovaniensium
BW	*Biblical World*
CBQ	*Catholic Biblical Quarterly*
ET	English translation
ETL	*Ephemerides Theologicae Lovanienses*
ExpT	*Expository Times*
JBL	*Journal of Biblical Literature*
JSNT	*Journal for the Study of the New Testament*
JSOT	*Journal for the Study of the Old Testament*
JTS	*Journal of Theological Studies*
NS	New series
NT	*Novum Testamentum*
NTS	*New Testament Studies*
PL	J. Migne, *Patrologia latina*
SNTS	Studiorum Novi Testamenti Societas
ST	*Studia theologica*
TDNT	*Theological Dictionary of the New Testament*
War	Josephus, *The Jewish War*
WUNT	Wissenschaftliche Untersuchungen zum Neuen Testament
ZNW	*Zeitschrift für die neutestamentliche Wissenschaft*

I

'Is This Not the Prophet?'

For an entire week between the day of his death, in November 1993, and the day of the funeral, the flag on my Cambridge college flew at half-mast as a mark of respect for my husband, David Stacey. That simple action of lowering the flag to half-mast was, I discovered, an amazingly evocative symbol, which not only conveyed instantly to all passers-by the news that a member of the college community had died, but also signified both the genuine sorrow of that community at his death and the affection and regard in which he was held.

Symbolic actions have a strange potency of their own: the ring given and received in a wedding ceremony, the water sprinkled on a child in baptism, the bread broken and shared at the eucharist; all point to a reality beyond the symbols themselves. In this book I want to explore the significance of Jesus' prophetic actions. It is an aspect of his life and work which has been comparatively neglected, for though the fact that Jesus performed prophetic actions has frequently been noted,[1] detailed discussion of Jesus as a prophet has usually concentrated on his words. But what he *did* was surely quite as important as what he *said*, and there has recently been increasing recognition of this.[2]

My opening illustration is a particularly apt one, because this book builds on my husband's work on prophetic drama in the Old Testament.[3] The last article he wrote before his death was on the Lord's Supper as prophetic drama,[4] and he had hoped to explore the theme further in a book. What I offer you now is not the book he would have written, but I know he would have approved of what I am trying to do, even though he might have disagreed over particular details. My investigation of this theme would certainly have been the better if I had been able to discuss it with him.

1. Prophetic actions in the Old Testament

We are accustomed to thinking of the Old Testament prophets as men and women who prophesied in spoken words. The very language we use – 'prophesy', 'foretell', 'forthtell' – suggests something oracular: the prophets proclaimed God's message to his people. But this message was sometimes proclaimed in actions as well as in oracles.[5] Moses, the first and greatest of the prophets, was honoured as the Law-giver, passing on to Israel the words of Yahweh which he heard on Sinai; but he was remembered also for what he did,[6] in bringing Israel out of captivity in Egypt. Samuel, too, is described as a prophet,[7] but he was remembered for his involvement in the events associated with the establishment of Israel's monarchy, rather than for anything he said. Similarly, the words of Elijah and Elisha were largely forgotten: what have been recorded in I and II Kings are accounts of the miracles which they are said to have performed. It is the later prophets whose words have been collected, edited and recorded, and who are thus known (somewhat inaccurately) as 'the writing prophets'. But even they are remembered in part for what they did, if only because some of them indulged in somewhat bizarre actions:[8] Isaiah walking around naked,[9] Jeremiah publicly smashing a pot,[10] Ezekiel eating a scroll[11] or lying, first on his left side, then on his right, for 390 days and 40 days respectively.[12] The record of their strange actions may well convey, better than anything else, the weird behaviour which characterized the prophets.

We are dealing here with actions of several different kinds. In the first place, we may distinguish between many of those attributed to the earlier prophets – to Moses, Elijah and Elisha in particular – which appear to have been what we would today call miraculous, and those which are associated more particularly with the later prophets, which we generally regard as symbolic. I doubt very much, however, whether those who first recorded these stories would have been happy with those descriptions. Perhaps it would be better to speak, on the one hand, of prophetic actions which mediate manifestations of divine power in events that bring with them either salvation or judgment, and on the other, of prophetic actions which point to a divine activity which cannot otherwise be observed at present. Examples of the former would be the story of Moses dividing the Red Sea, so ensuring the escape of the Israelites, but resulting in the destruction of the Egyptians;[13] Elijah raising a child to life;[14] and Elisha effecting the cleansing of Naaman.[15] Examples of the second group would be those strange actions of Isaiah, Jeremiah and Ezekiel to which I have already referred. Isaiah's nakedness symbolizes the coming humiliation of those nations which will be taken captive by Assyria;[16] Jeremiah's broken pot points to the coming destruction of Jerusalem;[17] the 390 days and 40 days that Ezekiel is commanded to spend lying on his left and right sides symbolize the punishment of Israel and Judah respectively. Sometimes these dramatic actions refer, not to future events, but to something that has already taken place or that is now taking place: when Ezekiel lay on his side, the time of punishment for Israel had already begun; when Hosea married Gomer and gave their children significant names, Israel was already unfaithful to Yahweh.[18] The prophetic actions in the first group are understood as leading to epiphanies: God is at work through the prophet, and what takes place is a manifestation of God's power. The actions in the second group are also manifestations – not direct manifestations of divine *power*, but manifestations of the divine *will*. Like prophetic oracles, these prophetic actions unveil God's purposes.

It is this second group of prophetic actions which my husband examined. The term he used of them, in preference to 'prophetic sign' or 'prophetic symbol', was 'prophetic drama'. These prophetic dramas are rather different from the symbolic action of my opening illustration, for whereas the flag flying at half-mast is a common symbol, whose significance is at once recognized by all who are familiar with a particular set of conventions, the prophets gave a unique meaning to actions which were not otherwise necessarily understood as conveying any particular significance. On the basis of his analysis David argued that the usual explanations of these dramatic actions were inadequate. They are not to be understood as mere visual aids – illustrations or 'acted parables' – intended to bring home to the prophet's audience in a memorable way the significance of his message. Nor should they be seen (like instrumental magic) as bringing about the events they symbolize: they did not *cause* things to happen![19] Rather these actions are dramatic presentations of the truth, an unveiling of what already exists in the divine intention. Prophetic oracle, prophetic drama, the historical happening to which they point, the written record left to us, are all different manifestations of an event whose origin and cause lie in the will of Yahweh. Drama, oracle, event and record are all, as it were, different modes of one reality. And what David said about prophetic actions can, I believe, be extended to apocalyptic vision, for here we have yet another mode, another manifestation of the divine purpose: the vision reveals to the recipient a reality that lies beyond time and place, disclosing not simply events which will one day take place on earth, but the truth as it already exists in heaven. God's purpose is thus revealed in different forms – in prophetic oracle,[20] dramatic action and apocalyptic vision – and each proclaims, in its own way, 'This is how things *are*'. Each of them is a manifestation of the underlying divine intention. Only if God's will changes – perhaps because men and women repent – can the future be different.[21] But that does not mean that the prophetic actions were mistaken. The oracle spoken in the name of the Lord, the prophetic drama and the vision, were all of them authentic because they represented a reality that had its being in God.[22]

Each kind of prophetic action that we have so far examined, then – both 'miracle' and 'prophetic drama' – is a manifestation of divine power. But whereas the miracle coincides with the divine action and brings either salvation or judgment with it, the prophetic drama points beyond itself to the purposes of God which are still to be worked out.

There is, however, yet a third kind of prophetic action. This is what we may call an 'authenticating miracle' or 'proof'. Now of course the miracles in our first group of prophetic actions were also – for those who comprehended their significance – 'proofs' of divine activity: Moses tells the terrified Israelites, pursued by Pharaoh's army, to stand firm and see the deliverance that God is going to perform.[23] But here it is the *deliverance*, rather than the *proof*, that is primary. In other cases, however, God gives a sign, either to the prophet or through the prophet, which serves to establish that he is the true God, that he is at work in this particular person, or that what the prophet says will come to pass. Thus Moses insists that he needs some kind of proof to persuade his people that he is God's instrument, and is given three signs: a staff that turns into a snake, a hand that becomes leprous, water that turns into blood.[24] Gideon is persuaded that he has been commissioned by Yahweh when fire miraculously consumes the sacrifice he has prepared,[25] and in much the same way Elijah's sacrifice is consumed by fire on Mt Carmel, leading Israel to acknowledge Yahweh as God.[26] Isaiah calls on Yahweh to move the sun backwards in the sky as a sign to Hezekiah that he will recover from his illness.[27] In all these cases, the sign involves direct divine intervention.

Some validating signs are less impressive. When Samuel anoints Saul king, he promises him a series of signs regarding the people he will meet on his way home.[28] When Jerusalem is under siege, Isaiah tells King Ahaz to ask for a sign, and when Ahaz refuses, Isaiah gives him one: a woman will have a child and name him Immanuel; before he reaches the age of discernment, the two kingdoms threatening Jerusalem will be left desolate.[29] The significance of all these signs is seen in the fact that the events which take place correspond exactly to what the prophet promised.[30] Fulfilment of a prophet's words – whether these refer directly to God's future activity of salvation or judgment, or to a sign that validates the prophet and his words – is an indication that the prophet has spoken in the name of the Lord.[31] But, unlike the other two kinds of prophetic action, they neither *effect* salvation or destruction nor *symbolize* God's purpose for his people.³² They are simply tangential proofs of the prophet's credentials.

2. The 'cessation of prophecy'

We turn now to the time of Jesus, and ask how prophetic figures of his day behaved. But first we must deal with a prior question: *were* there any prophetic figures at this time? It has frequently been maintained that the Jews of the Second Temple period believed that prophecy had ceased at some time in the past. The text that is most frequently quoted in support of this view is Tosefta Sotah 13.2: 'From the death of Haggai, Zechariah and Malachi, the latter prophets, the Holy Spirit ceased from Israel. But in spite of that she was allowed to hear a *bath-qol*.' Earlier texts have been said to demonstrate the same attitude: Zech. 13.2–6 seems to regard all claims to prophesy as false; Ps. 74.9 laments that 'We see no sign for us; there is no longer a prophet'; in I Macc. 4.44–46 Judas and his followers decide to tear down the polluted altar in the temple, and store the stones in a convenient place until a prophet should come to tell them what they should do with them; elsewhere in I Maccabees we find references to the time in the past when prophets ceased to appear in Israel³³ and to the time in the future when a trustworthy prophet should arise;³⁴ and in his treatise *Against Apion* Josephus speaks of 'the failure of the exact succession of the prophets'.³⁵

The idea that there was a general belief in the time of Jesus that prophecy had died out has recently been challenged, however, and it now seems clear that there was no such universal dogma. Rather there was a nostalgic belief that there were no longer any prophets *like the prophets of old*.³⁶ An important distinction should be made between the prophecy which was embodied in written texts and prophecy as an ongoing activity. With the growth of the canon, there were no longer any 'writing' prophets – and the only way in which the written word could be accepted as authoritative was by attributing it to an earlier prophet. In *that* sense, there were indeed no more prophets in the land. This is what Josephus is referring to, and this is why Tosefta Sotah distinguishes between the Holy Spirit and the *bath-qol*; the authority of the scriptures is regarded as being much greater than that of any subsequent oracle. But this did not mean that prophetic figures could not arise, and the passages that have been used to support the idea that prophecy had totally ceased need to be reassessed, since each of them refers to the particular situation in which it was written: the prophets who are condemned in Zechariah 13 are linked with the spirit of uncleanness and the idols, which will, with them, be removed from the land; the lament of Psalm 74 belongs to a period when Jerusalem has been devastated, and was probably written in Jerusalem at the time of the Exile – clearly by someone who was unaware of the activity of Ezekiel and Deutero-Isaiah in Babylon; the three references in I Maccabees acknowledge that there is no prophet at the moment, but confidently expect one to appear in the future.

The figure who is expected in I Maccabees is simply '*a* prophet'.[37] But at some stage hope for the future appears to have been more narrowly defined, and to have focussed on particular figures. This may well have been due in part to the failure of a recognized prophetic figure to emerge, for even if it is true that there was at this time no general belief that prophecy had ceased, it is nevertheless true also that there is no record of any prophet between Malachi and John the Baptist.[38] If there were prophets, then their names have not been remembered: they were certainly not of the same stature as the prophets of old. But whatever the reason, the expectation certainly became more precise. In the Qumran material, for example, we learn that the Community were expecting the coming of '*the* prophet', together with the Messiahs of Aaron and Israel.[39] Further evidence for this expectation is found in the Fourth Gospel, where there are at least three references to 'the prophet': in John 1.21, John the Baptist denies that he is the prophet, and in 6.14 and 7.40 the crowd concludes that Jesus is the prophet who is to come.[40] Do these references reflect pre-Christian expectations? And who *was* this prophet? Was he simply 'the eschatological prophet', or were expectations about him more clearly defined? The Qumran material gives us one further hint: in the short collection of texts known as the *Testimonia*[41] we find Old Testament texts which are interpreted as referring to the prophet and the two Messiahs, and one of the texts used of the prophet is Deut. 18.18f., where God says to Moses: 'I will raise up for Israel a prophet like you.'[42] The same text is appealed to in Acts 3.22 and 7.37. In the Fourth Gospel, the reference to the prophet in 6.14 follows the story of the miraculous feeding, which is interpreted in the rest of the chapter by a comparison of the bread given by Jesus with the manna provided for Israel in the wilderness through Moses: if Jesus is seen as 'the prophet who is to come into the world', it is clearly because he is 'like Moses'. We cannot, of course, necessarily rely on the Fourth Gospel[43] and the Acts of the Apostles as evidence for pre-Christian belief, but the Qumran text, together with the Samaritan belief in a future restorer who will be like Moses,[44] do suggest that in certain Jewish circles there was a hope that a prophet like Moses would appear.[45]

Another form of eschatological hope became associated with the figure of the returning Elijah. The first evidence for this is found in Mal. 4.5, where the Lord's messenger, who is to prepare his way (Mal. 3.1), is identified with Elijah. Apart from this passage and Sirach 48.10, which is based on it, there is no evidence for this particular expectation in the *pre-Christian* period. But it is attested in later Jewish literature and in the New Testament itself, where we find the identification of John the Baptist with the returning Elijah being affirmed in the Synoptics in sayings attributed to Jesus,[46] and denied in the Fourth Gospel, apparently by the Baptist himself.[47] The suggestion that Jesus himself might be the returning Elijah is found twice in the Synoptic story, and on each occasion it is attributed to the crowd, who suggest that he is John the Baptist raised from the dead, or Elijah, or some other prophet.[48] All this indicates that the idea of the return of Elijah was already current in first-century Judaism.

It would seem, then, that at the beginning of the first century

AD there had been no prophetic figure of any significance for many years. If one should now emerge, therefore, he would be seen, either as a great prophet like the prophets of old, or as an eschatological figure – in which case he could be envisaged either as *the* prophet like Moses promised in Deuteronomy 18 (as that passage was now understood) or as the returning Elijah, as foretold in Mal. 4.5.[49]

We return now to our initial question, and ask how prophetic figures of Jesus' day behaved. Those to be considered, apart from Jesus himself, are John the Baptist and the so-called 'sign prophets'.

3. John the Baptist

There is no doubt that John the Baptist was understood by all the evangelists to have been a prophet, and if their account is to be believed, he himself saw his own role as a prophetic one. His clothing and his food identified him as a prophet, and the former linked him, in particular, with Elijah.[50] The most significant thing about John was the activity which gave him his name – the fact that he baptized. So important was this that Mark describes him as 'preaching baptism'. Mark identifies this baptism as being a 'baptism of repentance for the forgiveness of sins'. The need for repentance is linked to the arrival of the One who is coming after John, who will baptize with the Holy Spirit. Matthew and Luke fill out this brief account of John's preaching, but they, too, understand his message to have been the need for repentance in preparation for the One who follows him. Those who respond to John's call are the true children of Abraham, members of God's covenant community.[51] In the Fourth Gospel, John's activity of baptizing is not described, though it is repeatedly referred to:[52] his baptism is not linked with repentance or forgiveness,[53] and John's only function is to point forward to Jesus.[54] When John is asked why he is baptizing, if he is neither the Messiah, nor Elijah, nor the prophet, he replies by linking his baptism with the arrival of the Coming One. In all the Gospels, therefore, John's baptism is interpreted as a preparation for the greater One who follows him.

Josephus, too, in his account of John in his *Antiquities*,[55] refers to him as 'the Baptist', but interprets his role very differently. John, he says, was a good man, who 'exhorted the Jews to lead righteous lives, to practise justice towards their fellows and piety towards God, and to come together for baptism.' He understands baptism, *not* as a means of gaining forgiveness for sins, but as a means of purifying the body, provided that the soul had already been cleansed by righteous behaviour. Josephus makes no reference here to Jesus, or to any other future figure, and there is no hint that John's function was preparatory.

Is it possible to discern the 'real' John the Baptist behind these various accounts – to discover how he himself saw his own role? On the one hand, we may well feel that the evangelists have distorted the evidence to some degree, in their eagerness to subordinate John to Jesus: this is certainly the case in the Fourth Gospel, where John's only answer to the question as to why he is baptising is to refer to the One who is coming after him.[56] But Josephus' account is also suspect: for if John's baptism had nothing to do with forgiveness, and served only to purify the body, how did it differ from normal ritual purifications? Why did the Jews flock to John to be baptized? And why should his baptism have been remembered as the key feature of his preaching?

If we look a little more carefully at Josephus' description of John's preaching, however, we find that it is closer to the synoptic account than we perhaps think. First, we notice his emphasis on John's ethical teaching – something which corresponds with an important element in Matthew and Luke. Secondly, he tells us that John exhorted the Jews 'to join in baptism'. We might have expected him to say simply 'to be baptized', but instead he uses a verb which signifies 'to come together'.[57] Here is a hint, at least, that John's baptism was seen as creating a new community, and thus had some kind of eschatological role. This would explain why Herod feared an uprising among the people, and so imprisoned John. Thirdly, it is important to realize that though Josephus denies that John thought of baptism itself as a means to obtain forgiveness for sins, he does at the same time emphasize that righteous behaviour was the necessary preliminary to baptism; the purification of the body was understood to symbolize the previous cleansing of the soul. We find a similar link between the two at Qumran in the *Community Rule*, which says of someone entering the community:

> He shall be cleansed from all his sins by the spirit of holiness uniting him to [God's] truth, and his iniquity shall be expiated by the spirit of uprightness and humility. And when his flesh is sprinkled with purifying water and sanctified by cleansing water, it shall be made clean by the humble submission of his soul to all the precepts of God.[58]

The most certain thing to emerge from all our sources is the fact that John baptized: he is remembered primarily for what he *did*. As far as his preaching is concerned, he clearly demanded righteousness, and this demand was linked in some way with the call to baptism. It seems probable that the demand for righteousness and the rite of baptism are both eschatological in their orientation: in other words, John proclaimed a coming judgment, which would bring punishment to the wicked and salvation to those who were truly God's people.

What, then, was the significance of John's baptism? We cannot discuss here the possible origin of this, whether in proselyte baptism or Qumran lustrations: neither provides an exact parallel, but each of them understands baptism as effecting purification from uncleanness. The metaphorical application of such a rite to moral cleansing is an obvious possibility, since sin was regarded as an uncleanness; it has its origin in the language of the prophets and the psalmists. 'Wash yourselves; make yourselves clean' thundered Isaiah, and his words were not simply a demand to his hearers to remove the blood that dripped from their hands, for he continues:

> Cease to do evil, learn to do good;
> seek justice, rescue the oppressed,
> defend the orphan, plead for the widow.[59]

The psalmist, pleading with God for forgiveness, prays:

> Purge me with hyssop, and I shall be clean;
> wash me, and I shall be whiter than snow. . . .
> Hide your face from my sins,
> and blot out all my iniquities.
> Create in me a clean heart, O God,
> and put a new and right spirit within me.[60]

And a passage in Ezekiel, describing what God is about to do, says:

> I will take you from the nations, and gather you from all the
> countries, and bring you into your own land. I will sprinkle
> clean water upon you, and you shall be clean from all your
> uncleannesses, and from all your idols I will cleanse you. A
> new heart I will give you, and a new spirit I will put within
> you, and I will remove from your body the heart of stone and
> give you a heart of flesh. I will put my spirit within you, and
> make you follow my statutes and observe my ordinances.[61]

These ideas would have been familiar to John and to his contemporaries.

When John appeared in the Jordan valley, preaching repentance and baptizing men and women in the river, he was seen as
a prophet, and his baptism would have been understood as a
prophetic action. Baptism with water signified a spiritual cleansing, and Mark is thus correct in describing it as a baptism for
the forgiveness of sins. But it is more than this. All four of our
evangelists are agreed in seeing John's baptism with water as
pointing forward to a baptism with Holy Spirit; Matthew and
Luke significantly add 'and fire', which suggests judgment. The
evangelists appear to *contrast* the two baptisms, because they
are anxious to stress the superiority of what Jesus does, but they
are not in fact seen as alternatives: rather, the baptism with

water demonstrates the inevitability of the baptism with Spirit. John's baptism with water is thus a prophetic sign that the One who follows him will baptize with Holy Spirit.[62] John's message is addressed to all Israel, and the fact that the whole of Judaea and all the inhabitants of Jerusalem respond to his call and are baptized[63] points to the coming judgment of all God's people, when the righteous will be cleansed with the Holy Spirit and purged with fire,[64] and when the wicked will be destroyed. Like Isaiah's nakedness or Jeremiah's pot, John's baptism is *a dramatic representation of what will inevitably follow*. This perhaps explains why baptism was taken over by the Christian movement and why it is so firmly linked with the gift of the Spirit in early Christian tradition; although they are presented as alternatives in the tradition about John, baptism in water and in Spirit in fact belong together: the former is the symbol, or sign, of the latter.[65]

4. The 'sign prophets'

We turn now to the prophetic figures whom modern scholars often refer to as 'sign prophets',[66] a description which is not entirely accurate, since there is no record of any of them actually performing a sign; they did, however, *promise* to perform signs. Our knowledge of them comes from Josephus, and all of them belong to the period AD 44–70 – that is, *after* the ministry of Jesus. Nevertheless, they give us some idea of what a prophetic figure in the first century would be expected to do. Josephus regards them all as impostors.[67] Two of them are said to have claimed to be prophets and to have promised to perform specific signs (though the term *sēmeion* is not used of either): the first is Theudas, who is mentioned briefly in Acts 5.36, and who appeared in AD 44 or soon after and led his followers to the River Jordan, promising that the river would part; the group fell into the hands of the Romans, who slaughtered some and captured the rest.[68] There was also an unnamed Egyptian, who led his followers to the Mount of Olives in the time of Felix (AD 52–60), claiming that the walls of Jerusalem would fall down at his command.[69] Again, they were routed by the Romans. Each of these miracles, had it occurred, would have paralleled events in the Exodus story, and would have been in itself an act of deliverance.

Other prophetic figures are described as promising 'wonders and signs': Josephus refers to 'impostors and deceivers' who led a mob into the desert in the fifties, promising them 'signs of deliverance'.[70] During the siege of Jerusalem in AD 70, another unnamed prophet told the people to go to the temple to await the 'signs of deliverance'.[71] In the seventies, the Zealot Jonathan led his followers into the desert, promising to show them 'signs and apparitions'.[72] Once again, the movement was overcome by Rome. In all these accounts, the prophets are said to have promised *sēmeia*, signs, though what exactly these signs were to be is nowhere stated.[73] Because two of them went into the desert, it is often assumed that these men promised to perform miracles such as Moses is said to have performed there, but in a recent book Rebecca Gray has argued that when Josephus is referring to the Exodus tradition he uses the word *sēmeia* in a very specific way.[74] She points out that, whereas the LXX uses that term of the great miracles of the Exodus – the plagues, the parting of the sea, the provision of food and water in the wilderness – Josephus uses it only of the three miracles taught to Moses at the burning bush,[75] miracles which he was to use when he needed to persuade the Hebrews or Pharaoh that he had been sent by God: he learned how to turn his staff into a serpent, how to turn his hand white and return it to normality, and how to turn water into blood.[76]

In other words, when Josephus uses the word *sēmeion*, he is thinking of what I earlier termed an 'authenticating miracle' or 'proof'. The men who promised such signs would be attempting to demonstrate that they had divine authority for their mission. The miracles promised by Theudas and the Egyptian, on the other hand, who declared that the waters of Jordan would part and the walls of Jerusalem fall down, would have been direct manifestations of divine power – prophetic actions of the kind which I earlier called 'epiphanies'.[77]

What unites all these various figures is the promise to perform certain actions: it is because they fail to do so that they are clearly impostors.[78]

5. Jesus

Finally, we turn to Jesus himself. That Jesus, like John, was regarded in his own day as a prophet seems to be beyond doubt. Even though the evangelists clearly regarded Jesus as far more than a prophet, and considered his designation as such to be inadequate, they include many traces of a tradition that saw him in this light. Mark twice sums up popular reaction to Jesus by telling us that he was regarded by his contemporaries as some kind of prophet, though what kind of prophet he might be was uncertain. He might be a previous prophet returned: either John the Baptist raised from the dead, or Elijah, or one of the other prophets;[79] or he might be a *new* prophet, like one of the prophets of old – that is, of equal stature with them.[80] These summary statements are supported by other passages: the crowd describes him as 'the prophet Jesus from Nazareth' in Matt. 21.11,[81] and declares in Luke 7.16 that 'a great prophet has risen among us'; two of his followers refer to him as 'a prophet mighty in deed and word' in Luke 24.19. He is dismissed as a false prophet in Luke 7.39, and mocked as such in Mark 14.65.[82] Jesus is said to have referred to himself in terms of a prophet in Mark 6.4 and in Luke 4.24 and 13.33.[83] The Fourth Gospel, too, records popular opinion that Jesus was a prophet;[84] on two occasions in this Gospel, Jesus is said to be '*the* prophet'.[85] In Acts, both Peter and Stephen are said to have applied to Jesus the prophecy in Deut. 18.18 that God would raise up another prophet like Moses.[86] The famous passage in the Talmud which refers to Jesus' death accuses him of practising sorcery and leading Israel astray. It tells us also that although Jesus was hanged on the eve of Passover, he was in fact found worthy of death by stoning because he was a deceiver, to whom Deut. 13.8 applies: Deut. 13.1–11 is a warning against false prophets who deceive the people.[87]

In a famous essay published as long ago as 1930, C.H. Dodd set out fifteen features of Jesus' ministry which would have led the people to regard him as a prophet.[88] Among these are his authoritative teaching, his sense of calling and possession of divine insight, and his symbolic actions. When we look a little more closely at the passages I have just listed, we see that all of them relate to one or other of these themes. The sayings attributed to Jesus himself in Mark 6 and Luke 4 and 13 speak of his own call and the rejection of that call by the people, as does Acts 7. Three of the passages, Mark 14.65, Luke 7.39 and John 4.19, suggest that Jesus was *expected* to act with prophetic insight, even though – in the view of the bystanders – he failed to do so. Matt. 21.46, John 7.40 and Acts 3.22 are in a context which refers to Jesus' teaching. Luke 24.19 describes Jesus as a 'prophet mighty in deed and word'. But the vast majority – Mark 6.4; 6.15 and parallels; 8.28 and parallels; Matt. 21.11; Luke 4.24, 7.16 and 24.19; John 6.14 and 9.17 – refer to or are juxtaposed with accounts of what Jesus *did*. Jesus was regarded as a prophet, not simply because he *spoke* like a prophet, but because he *acted* like a prophet. We have good reason, then, for looking more closely at his actions, and in particular at those actions which can be described as prophetic 'signs' or 'dramas'.

II

'No Sign Shall Be Given Them'

It is well known that in the Synoptic Gospels, the term *sēmeia*, signs, is normally used in a negative sense: Jesus is presented as refusing to perform signs. The Fourth Gospel is another matter – and we must return to consider that in more detail in a later chapter – but for the moment we concentrate on the Synoptic tradition, except to notice when the Fourth Gospel backs it up.

On two occasions in Matthew, Jesus rebuffs the demand of his opponents that he show them a sign. One of the stories is found also in Mark, the other in Luke.[1] The details of the stories vary, but all three evangelists describe Jesus' opponents as testing (or tempting) him.[2] In all three Gospels, Jesus is said to have denounced the generation who demand a sign, and to have declared that it would not be given one – apart, that is (according to Matt. 12.39 and 16.4 and Luke 11.29) from the sign of Jonah.

It is clear that all three evangelists understand the sign which is being demanded to refer to some kind of authenticating miracle which would confirm Jesus' authority: the signs which are required of Jesus are miracles of the kind which Moses performed in Egypt, for which Josephus also, as we have seen, uses the word *sēmeia*. It is signs of this kind which, according to Mark 13 and Matthew 24, will be used by false prophets, in their attempts to deceive the elect.[3] The demand for Jesus to perform such a miracle indicates that he was being seen in the category of a prophet (albeit a false one).[4] But *why* was he being seen as a prophet? The answer to that is apparently that he had already been *behaving* like a prophet, for when we look at the context of these various traditions we discover that in every case

the demand follows *after* a miracle.[5] In Matt. 12.22–24 Jesus
exorcises a demon, and is accused of doing so in the name of
Beelzebul; Jesus refutes the accusation, but in v.38 he is asked
for a sign from heaven, presumably to prove that his authority
also comes from heaven. In Luke 11.14f., an account of the
same exorcism and accusation leads immediately to the same
request. Jesus ignores it, but deals with the accusation about
Beelzebul. Then in v.29 he picks up their demand for a sign
and rebuts it. In Mark 8.1–10 and Matt. 15.32–39, Jesus is
said to have fed a large crowd; immediately afterwards,
Pharisees demand a sign. The link between the feeding and the
demand is backed up by the Fourth Evangelist, for he records a
similar incident after his version of the feeding.[6] All four of our
evangelists, therefore, juxtapose a miracle of Jesus with a
demand that he perform a sign, so underlining the failure of the
religious leaders to see the significance of what Jesus has already
done. For those with faith, miracles *are* signs of God's activity.[7]
What is being demanded of Jesus – and what he refuses to
perform – is an *authenticating* miracle, which will show that his
authority comes from God, and not from Beelzebul.

1. The sign of Jonah

But in three of these narratives, Jesus' opponents *are* promised a
sign, namely the sign of Jonah.[8] This was certainly not the kind
of 'authenticating miracle' that Jesus' opponents had in mind –
but what was it? Matthew 16 offers no explanation of this
mysterious sign, but in Matthew 12 and Luke 11 it is taken to
be Jonah himself; Matthew 12 interprets it of the resurrection –
which is clearly a *post eventum* explanation – while Luke 11
refers to Jonah as 'a sign to the Ninevites' without further
explanation. Presumably Luke understood the saying to mean
that Jesus, like Jonah, is proclaiming judgment – not to the
Ninevites, but to Israel.[9] But why should *Jonah's* preaching be
mentioned – rather than that of any of the great prophets sent
to Israel, who also proclaimed Yahweh's judgment? Is it
perhaps because Jonah was said to come from Galilee?[10] If so,

the reference could be an ironic one, since in Jesus' case this apparently precluded him, in some eyes, from being considered a prophet at all! That tradition is found only in John, however, and probably refers to the eschatological prophet.[11] The truly remarkable thing about Jonah, however, was that he was sent to *preach* to Gentiles, and there is no hint in any of the Gospels that Jesus preached to Gentiles: his ministry appears to have been confined to Jews. Moreover, the Ninevites repented at Jonah's preaching, whereas the point in all three of these passages is that the present generation is wicked, and will surely be condemned. And in what sense could Jonah's message be described as a *sign*? The saying itself, found in three different forms, may well go back to Jesus, but the evangelists were clearly baffled as to its meaning, and so are the commentators!

So what *was* the sign of Jonah? The phrase *to sēmeion Iōna* can be understood in three ways. First, it might be taken to mean a sign given *by* Jonah; there is, however, nothing in the biblical story to suggest that Jonah performed any action which could be described as a 'sign'. The only significant things that Jonah did were to run away, to preach (reluctantly), and to sulk when he was successful. Secondly, it can be understood as a sign given *to* Jonah. There are two unusual features in the story of Jonah, either of which could qualify to be considered as a 'sign given to Jonah'. The first is the account of Jonah's adventures in chapters 1 and 2: Jonah, attempting to escape from God's call to preach in Nineveh, is hurled into the sea during a storm by his terrified shipmates, but God conveniently arranges for a large fish to swallow him and convey him to dry land. This remarkable rescue from death is the feature picked up by Matthew in 12.40. But in the story of Jonah the 'sign' is directed to the prophet, not (as in Matthew) to others; as a result of this experience, Jonah is persuaded that he cannot escape God's call, and in that sense, the event could be interpreted as an 'authenticating miracle' – intended, unusually, to persuade the prophet himself, not his audience, of the genuineness of his mission. The story is certainly no arbitrary sign of authority of the kind demanded from Jesus by the Pharisees,[12] and is much more properly described as a miracle of deliverance which enables Jonah to carry out his task. It is difficult to see how the notion that this event was a sign given *to Jonah* could be relevant to Jesus' situation.

The other unusual feature in the story of Jonah is the account of the climbing gourd which sprang up and provided him with welcome shade, but which was destroyed in a morning. This is clearly seen as 'a sign to Jonah', though once again, this is not a tangential 'sign from heaven' to authenticate his prophetic calling, but more akin to a 'prophetic sign', even though it is performed by God himself. Unlike prophetic signs, however, the withering of the gourd signifies the *original* purpose of the Lord, which has now been abandoned. The fate of the gourd is interpreted to Jonah as a sign of the destruction with which God had threatened Nineveh, but which she had escaped through repentance. But now, say Matthew and Luke, Nineveh will witness against *this* generation and ensure its condemnation,[13] and the only sign given them ought therefore to be a sign of destruction. What, then, could this sign be, and when would it be given? Was there at some stage a link with the story of the barren fig tree, which is recorded by Luke as a parable, but which is understood by both Matthew and Mark to refer to an actual tree, which, like the gourd, withered in an instant?[14] Tempting as this explanation is, I cannot find any trace of it in the tradition! But there is no doubt that the story of the barren fig tree was understood as a prophetic sign, and we must return to it later.

The third possible interpretation of the phrase *to sēmeion Iōna* is that the genitive is one of apposition, and that the sign is Jonah himself; this is the way in which it is understood in both Matthew 12 and Luke 11.[15] Matthew compares Jonah's three days and nights in the fish with Jesus' three days and nights in the tomb. His interpretation points to what was by his time the obvious link between the two stories: Jonah was delivered by God from what looked like certain death, and the Son of man will be saved in a similarly dramatic way. Since this is unlikely to be a dominical explanation, however, it cannot help us to understand what Jesus himself might have meant by 'the sign of Jonah'. Luke describes Jonah as 'a sign to the Ninevites', and compares him with what the Son of man will be to 'this generation'. The only hint as to how he understands Jonah to have been a sign is found in the reference to his preaching in v.32. Yet the link in Luke's comparison seems thin, for Jonah preached judgment to the Ninevites, and the result was their repentance, whereas Jesus proclaimed forgiveness, and the consequence was judgment! Indeed, it has to be said that Jonah is anything but a good parallel to Jesus: Jonah was disobedient, and refused the call of God, whereas Jesus is depicted by the evangelists as obedient and well-pleasing to God; Jonah proclaimed judgment, and was resentful of God's mercy, whereas Jesus proclaimed salvation, and wept over the people's refusal to respond; Jonah's preaching met with total success, since the Ninevites all repented, whereas Jesus' ministry appeared to end in failure. It seems unlikely that Jesus himself would have seen Jonah as a role-model.

In some ways, Jonah's story runs parallel, not to that of Jesus, but to that of the Ninevites, since he, like them, deserved to perish and was saved from destruction by God's mercy. In that sense Jonah himself might well be described as a 'sign' to the Ninevites – a sign that God would have mercy on them if they repented, and save them from destruction, just as he had saved Jonah from death. But in what sense could Jonah be described as a sign to the *present* generation? Is the 'sign' that Jesus now offers his contemporaries also a positive one – a restoration which is a token of God's mercy? Is it perhaps the salvation that is already at work through him? Not, indeed, in his own resurrection from death (though that is how Matthew 12 interprets it), but in the fact that through the miracles of healing worked by Jesus, God is restoring men and women to life? In its simplest form, in Matthew 16, the saying could mean just that.

The sign has already been given, but Jesus' enemies have no eyes to see it, as the incident immediately before this one in both Matthew 12 and Luke 11 makes plain.[16] But why should this comparatively straightforward idea be described by the enigmatic phrase 'the sign of Jonah'? The use of this phrase suggests that we need to think of something more specific.

Does the extra-biblical tradition about Jonah perhaps have light to throw on our problem? There are two Jewish texts, each of which dates from approximately the first century AD, which may be relevant. The first is *The Lives of the Prophets*, which (in common with other Jewish writings[17]) identifies Jonah with the son of the widow of Zarephath, and so links Jonah's escape from death with a story about a miraculous resurrection.[18] This text says of Jonah that when he returned to Judah, he foretold the destruction of Jerusalem: 'And he gave a *portent* concerning Jerusalem and the whole land, that whenever they should see a stone crying out piteously the end was at hand. And whenever they should see all the Gentiles in Jerusalem, the entire city would be razed to the ground.'[19] The other text is the homily *De Jona*, where Jonah's rescue is described as making him a 'sign' of rebirth.[20] These passages suggest that the notion of the 'sign of Jonah' may have been one that was already known to Jesus' contemporaries. The ideas in these texts are parallel to the two interpretations of the 'sign' in Matthew and Luke: on the one hand, we have Jonah himself being seen, because of his dramatic rescue from death, as a sign of salvation and new life, and on the other, we find the preacher who proclaimed the imminent destruction of Nineveh prophesying the destruction of his own people and giving a portent of coming judgment to Israel. In addition, both Matthew and Luke draw a comparison between the Ninevites who repented at the preaching of Jonah and the contemporaries of Jesus, who do not.[21]

One interesting feature of Jonah's prophecy in *The Lives of the Prophets* is that it refers to two signs: the stone which cries out piteously is a portent that the end is at hand; the presence of Gentiles in Jerusalem is an indication that the city is to be razed to the ground. Do these two signs refer to the same event? There is an intriguing parallel with the eschatological discourse in the Synoptic Gospels, a passage which may well be relevant to our enquiry, since here we have another request for a sign – this time from Jesus' own disciples: 'When will these things happen?

And what will be *the sign* that all these things are about to be fulfilled?'[22] Their question follows Jesus' prophecy of the destruction of the temple, but his reply deals also with the events leading up to 'the end'.[23] The predictions refer to two stages: first (in Matthew and Mark), the abomination of desolation (which certainly involves the presence of Gentiles in the temple) will indicate that Jerusalem is about to be destroyed; in Luke, the armies encircling Jerusalem show that her destruction is near, and that she will be trampled underfoot by the Gentiles.[24] Second, portents in heaven are the sign that the Son of man is about to appear.[25] As for the stone that cries piteously, we may compare Luke 19.40, where Jesus refers to the stones which are ready to cry out to welcome him to Jerusalem. This is certainly a very different idea from the 'piteous' cry in *The Lives*, and yet it is immediately followed by Jesus' lament over Jerusalem and his declaration that the time of her destruction by her enemies is near (vv.41–44).

Are our various texts drawing on common tradition? Are the similarities accidental? Or has one influenced the other? And if so, which is the earlier? It is difficult to make any positive pronouncement on this matter. What can be said is that the extra-biblical material helps us to understand why there should be references in the eschatological discourse to portents of the destruction of Jerusalem and of the end of all things, and why the saying about 'the sign of Jonah' should have been interpreted in two such very different ways by Matthew and Luke. But none of this helps us to understand the saying in the context of Jesus' own ministry.

Additional Note on Portents

In *The Lives of the Prophets*, Jonah is said to have given a portent (*teras*) of the end of Jerusalem. In fact, as we have seen, he gives two; when certain events take place, the end is at hand and Jerusalem will be destroyed. These portents are quite different from the kind of 'authenticating' sign that Jesus is asked to do. They are not performed by the prophet at all, though they are prophesied by him. In this particular case, one event (a stone shrieking) is presumably super-natural, the other (the presence of Gentiles in Jerusalem) is not. These portents will indicate that some other future event, also prophesied, is about to happen.

Portents of great events are referred to from time to time in the Gospels. We have noted already the response that Jesus is said to have given to the demands for a sign of Jerusalem's destruction: a prophecy that the abomination of desolation will stand where he ought not, and (in Luke) the saying about the armies encircling Jerusalem. There follows a warning about supernatural portents in heaven, which will mark the coming of the Son of man. Supernatural portents accompany the crucifixion, and are clearly understood to be indications of its significance: the darkness at midday,[26] the rending of the temple curtain[27] and the resurrection of the dead.[28] Another (the appearance and movement of a star) is described as marking Jesus' birth in Matt. 2.1–10. These various portents are all indications that some great event has taken place or is about to take place.

2. The sign of John?

Since all explanations seem inadequate, it is tempting to adopt the suggestion made by various earlier commentators that the saying in Matt. 12.39//Matt. 16.4//Luke 11.29 originally referred, not to the sign of Jonah but to the sign of *John* – i.e. the Baptist. In this case the sign given to this generation must be the *baptism* of John, since baptism was John's distinguishing feature.[29] The sign had been given, but its significance had been ignored by those who now ask Jesus for another. Although this suggestion has generally been dismissed, it would certainly make excellent sense of the saying (without its Matthean elabo-ration) if we are right in understanding John's baptism as a prophetic action which looked forward to the future judgment, and so signified both salvation and destruction. This 'sign' has already been given: future judgment is inevitable. Those who now respond to Jesus' proclamation will be saved, and those who reject it will be condemned.

This interpretation fits well with another saying in which Jesus, when challenged about his authority, appeals to the baptism of John which, it is clearly implied, was 'from heaven':[30] on that occasion John's baptism is, as it were, offered by Jesus as an 'authenticating sign' to his opponents. Needless, to say, it was not the kind of sign they either wanted or would recognize! In all three Synoptics, this challenge takes place in the temple, where Jesus is teaching, and follows his entry into Jerusalem, his 'cleansing' of the temple and (in Matthew and Mark) the cursing of the fig tree. Presumably it is these events that are referred to when the Jewish leaders ask about his authority to do 'these things' – events which all signify the judgment brought by Jesus, a judgment which means salvation for those who respond and destruction for those who reject him. If I was right in interpreting John's baptism as a prophetic sign pointing forward to Jesus' baptism with the Spirit which purges, renews and destroys, then Jesus' appeal to John's baptism as the 'authentication' of his actions in Jerusalem is understandable.

But is this a satisfactory explanation of Jesus' saying about the sign? Should we simply substitute 'John' for 'Jonah'? The obvious difficulty with this solution is that all three versions of the saying refer, not to John, but to Jonah, and their united evidence cannot so easily be dismissed. The fact that both Matthew 12 and Luke 11 then add further sayings about Jonah seems to confirm that this first saying referred to Jonah from the very beginning. But does this mean that we have to abandon the reference to John? I suggest not. It is clear that for the saying to make any sense, 'Jonah' has to be interpreted as a reference to a prophetic figure who addresses *this* generation.[31] Some kind of 'translation' is necessary, and there are two possibilities: Jesus and John. 'The sign of Jonah' can, in fact, refer to a sign performed by John just as easily as to a sign performed by Jesus. To be sure, both Matthew 12 and Luke 11 assumed that the parallel was with Jesus himself – referred to as 'the Son of man' – and their assumption is understandable, since it is *Jesus* who has been asked to provide a sign of *his* authority: in effect, they understand the sign of Jonah to be one which is now re-enacted in the person of Jesus. Their attempts to draw that parallel are, however, very different, and Matthew's, at least, is certainly a later construction. But were they correct in the assumption? It is arguable that Jesus was here making use of a word-play on the very similar names 'Jonah' and 'John', and that the sign of Jonah *for this generation* was therefore given by John the Baptist.[32] The names were so alike as to have been at times interchangeable.[33] It has, indeed, been argued that the saying which follows immediately after this one in Luke (v.30) represents a word-play on the two names: 'as Jonah was a sign to the Ninevites, so will John be to this generation.'[34] Certainly the similarity in names might have been enough to suggest that the new Jonah is John, whose baptism was the sign (for those who had eyes to see) that what was now taking place in Jesus was the work of God. The fact that Jonah had proclaimed judgment, and that this had led to the salvation of the Ninevites from punishment, would certainly make a comparison between Jonah and John highly appropriate, for John had demanded repentance before the coming judgment, and he was followed by One who offered salvation.

If Jesus drew a comparison of this kind between Jonah and John, however, the 'sign of Jonah' must have been in some way comparable to John's baptism. Could it perhaps be, after all, a reference to the gourd? Certainly the gourd was an enigmatic sign, representing both God's mercy and his condemnation of sin: it brought Jonah comfort, but then was destroyed. Jonah's preaching (like John's) proved to be a truly eschatological event, since it confronted the people with a pronouncement of condemnation, which was expected to lead to destruction; but because the Ninevites repented, God's original message of judgment had been transformed into a message of mercy. John's baptism is similarly ambivalent: it points forward to a baptism 'in Holy Spirit and fire' – a baptism which brings both destruction and renewal. And though Jesus' proclamation of God's Kingdom is embodied in stories which stress God's mercy and in miracles which enact his salvation, yet when it is rejected, then judgment is inevitable. And so the men of Nineveh will rise up at the judgment and condemn this present generation. The story of the gourd represents exactly the choice presented to Jesus' hearers, the choice to respond or to reject, to be saved or to be condemned.

Yet the other 'sign' given to Jonah – his escape from drowning and his 'rebirth' – is even more appropriate to the figure of John. Many of the early Fathers interpret the sign of Jonah as a reference to Jonah's rescue from death at sea,[35] though (like Matthew) they mostly go on to explain it in terms of Christ's death and resurrection. But the throwing of Jonah overboard, and his subsequent escape from the fish, again correspond to the ambivalence of John's baptism, signifying destruction on the one hand and renewal, following repentance, on the other. Moreover the fact that Jonah is cast into the water, to emerge from the water to a new life, makes the parallel with John's baptism particularly apt. Jonah was submerged beneath the water's surface to face what seemed like certain death, only to be saved by what appeared to be an agent of destruction. His experience in a sense symbolizes that of the Ninevites, heading for destruction, yet saved by God's grace when they repent. John's baptism, also, involved being submerged under the water and rising to a new life, and it pointed forward to a baptism with Holy Spirit which would purge and destroy, as well as renew: according to the Q tradition, this would be effected through wind and fire, winnowing-fan and shovel, the elements and tools of salvation and destruction. Acceptance of John's baptism meant submitting to God's judgment, as Jonah (and the Ninevites) had done. It was hardly surprising if Paul saw the rite of baptism as a symbol of death and new life: others before him may well have done the same. If the sign given to 'this generation' is in fact the baptism of John, what could be more appropriate than to refer to it as 'the sign of Jonah'? For Jonah's descent beneath the water had symbolized destruction, and his re-emergence had symbolized salvation.

If this is the correct interpretation, then it is hardly surprising, either that Mattthew interpreted the saying as a reference to Jesus' own rescue from death, or that in the early church, the story of Jonah's rescue from the sea and from the fish was much used on tombs and in the catacombs, indicating the new life that came to them through Christ.[36] Nor is it surprising that Luke interpreted the sign of Jonah as a reference to the coming judgment of Israel. The two evangelists have picked up different aspects of the one image, an image which points both to the destruction of the disobedient and to the salvation of those who repent.[37]

If Jesus was in fact referring to Jonah *alias* John the Baptist in this passage, then we have an interesting parallel with the saying in Mark 9.11–13//Matt. 17.10–12, where a similar identification takes place when, without any explanation, the Baptist is referred to as Elijah. Whether or not that particular saying goes back to Jesus is debatable, but it proves to be doubly relevant to our enquiry since, for the evangelists at least, John is once again understood to be a sign. This time, it is his death that is seen as a 'prophetic sign' (endured, rather than enacted, by the prophet) of what is certainly going to happen to the Son of man: if Elijah (alias John) has been put to death, the same fate will inevitably befall the one who comes after him. There is a further interesting similarity between the two passages in the fact that in both cases the reference to the Old Testament prophet is enigmatic: if we are puzzled by the reference to the sign of Jonah, we are equally puzzled by Mark's reference to what the scriptures have to say about the sufferings of Elijah, since there is no specific reference to such suffering in the Old Testament.

But there is another hint that John may be relevant to the sign of Jonah in the context of the saying, where we find reference to the Holy Spirit. In Luke, the demand for a sign follows a section in which Jesus teaches his disciples to pray, and which ends with the statement that God will give the Holy Spirit to those who ask him.[38] In both Matthew and Luke, the demand for a sign is linked with Jesus' refutation of his opponents' charge that he is exorcising unclean spirits in the power of Satan. In Matthew, the demand follows the dispute, while in Luke, the demand immediately precedes the dispute, and is only dealt with when Jesus has shown the absurdity of the allegations. This suggests that both evangelists (or the tradition before them) saw a link between the demand for a sign and the dispute about the exorcisms. The healings that Jesus is performing are, we are told, being done in the power of the Holy Spirit (or by the finger of God), not Satan.[39] For those with eyes to see, the miracles are in effect themselves 'signs' that God is at work. Luke's reference to 'the finger of God' is particularly interesting, since this phrase is used in Ex. 8.19, when the Egyptian magicians fail to repeat the miracle of creating gnats and acknowledge that God himself is at work in what Moses and Aaron are doing. If Jesus is asked for proof of his claim that he is working in the power of God, what more appropriate witness could there be than John the Baptist, whose baptism was the sign of the coming baptism in Spirit? The argument used to counter the challenge in the temple[40] is as relevant and appropriate here as it is there.

There is, perhaps, some evidence that the saying about the sign of Jonah was once understood as a reference to John in the sayings which follow it in Matt. 12.41f.//Luke 11.31f. In the Matthaean order, we have a saying about the men of Nineveh condemning the present generation, followed by a parallel saying about the queen of the South. The men of Nineveh repented at the preaching of Jonah, and the queen of the South came from the ends of the earth to hear the wisdom of Solomon. The implication is that the present generation has ignored both the preaching of the modern Jonah and the wisdom of the modern Solomon. In both cases, the Jews of Jesus' time are contrasted unfavourably with Gentiles who responded to God's word. Commentators usually identify the 'something' which is greater than Jonah with the 'something' which is greater than Solomon, and assume that both sayings refer to Jesus. But there is surely an implicit *contrast* between the proclamation which leads to *repentance* and the wisdom which *attracts* someone 'from the ends of the earth'. All three Synoptic evangelists describe John as preaching repentance,[41] which suggests that the first saying may in fact refer to him, and to his work of baptism: in Mark and Luke he is said to preach a *baptism* of repentance.[42] But why should Jesus be compared with Solomon, suggesting that his activity is to be understood in terms of wisdom? Since Solomon was the son of David, there is possibly a hint that a greater son has now arisen, but part of the explanation is perhaps to be found in Josephus' description of Solomon's wisdom in *Antiquities* 8.42–9, where outstanding examples of his wisdom are said to be his ability to compose odes and parables and his skill in expelling demons and healing the sick.[43] The description is reminiscent of Jesus, for it is both by his teaching in parables and by his exorcisms and healings that he proclaims the Kingdom of God.

If in fact the 'something'[44] which is greater than Jonah is John's summons to repentance, and the 'something' which is greater than Solomon is Jesus' proclamation of the Kingdom of God,[45] we have an interesting parallel to Jesus' words elsewhere about the failure of men and women to respond both to John's message and to his own. They are like children who have failed either to mourn or to dance:

> For John came neither eating nor drinking, and they say, 'He has a demon'; the Son of man came eating and drinking, and they say, 'Look, a glutton and a drunkard, a friend of tax collectors and sinners!'[46]

Intriguingly, this passage ends in another reference to wisdom, even more enigmatic than that in Matt. 12.42 and Luke 11.31. In Luke, the saying appears to refer to the purpose of God, which will ultimately be vindicated by the response of those who accept it.[47] In Matthew, wisdom is vindicated by her 'works', a statement which appears to be a reference to the miracles of Jesus:[48] this interpretation of the saying corresponds with the idea that he embodies wisdom expressed in 12.41f.[49]

The ministries of John and Jesus are not simply set in parallel here, but are clearly linked.[50] This is underlined by the fact that these sayings about people's failure to respond to their preaching come in the context of others which are relevant to our theme. The section begins with the message of John to Jesus enquiring whether or not he is the expected Coming One. In reply, Jesus refers to his miracles of healing – in Luke, indeed, he heals various people before responding in words. Here we find Jesus *offering* John 'authenticating' signs of his identity! But they are not mere 'proofs' of the kind offered to Pharaoh by Moses: rather, they are signs that the Kingdom of God is bursting into the world. We are then told that Jesus made various comments about John's own ministry, including the quotation from Ex. 23.20–Mal. 3.1, which speaks of the messenger who prepares the way of one who follows him: here John is identified as Jesus' forerunner, and the ministries of John and Jesus are thus linked.

The idea that John is Jesus' forerunner is, of course, to some extent redactional. Mark, in his use of *paradidōmi* of John in 1.14, sees this as an omen of Jesus' own handing over, and later tells the story of John's death in such a way as to point forward to that of Jesus. Luke, in his opening chapters, clearly understands the stories of John and Jesus to be unfolding in tandem. Matthew identifies John with Elijah.[51] John sees the sole function of the Baptist as to point forward to Jesus.[52] But if my interpretation of John's baptism in Chapter 1 is correct, then his action did point forward to something else, and if my understanding of Jesus' words in the temple[53] is right, Jesus saw that baptism as a 'sign' of what he himself was doing. The material in Matthew 11 // Luke 7 and Matthew 17 // Mark 9 is consistent with this. And if the 'sign of Jonah' is indeed a reference to John, that, too, fits into the same pattern. There is sufficient evidence to suggest that Jesus himself understood John's ministry to be pointing forward to his own.

3. The refusal to perform signs

Whatever explanation we give for the sign of Jonah, the evangelists are agreed that Jesus refused to offer a 'sign' in the sense of an authenticating miracle. The 'exception' is not a real exception since, whatever it is, it is not an authenticating miracle, but most probably something that has already taken place, whose significance has not been understood.

One further example from the Synoptics of Jesus' refusal to perform authenticating miracles should be noted. This is found in the story of Jesus' temptation by Satan. The first temptation,

to turn stones into bread, is apparently understood by both
Matthew and Luke to be to use his power for his own benefit,
since they both comment that Jesus was hungry.[54] The suggestion that he should throw himself down from the pinnacle of the
temple, however, is clearly a temptation to give the people a sign
that would establish his identity and authority. This is presumably the kind of sign which is demanded by Jesus' opponents later in the Gospels, and it is no accident that the verb
peirazō, used of Satan's activity in the temptation narratives by
all three Synoptic evangelists, is used also in three of the four
accounts of the demands of Jesus' opponents for a sign.[55] The
devil's suggestion is dismissed by Jesus with a quotation from
Deut. 6.16 which uses the same verb: 'You shall not test/tempt
the Lord your God.' The words in Deuteronomy refer to the
incident at Massah, where the Israelites doubt God's ability to
give them water,[56] and the demand for proofs in the Gospels
stems from a similar lack of trust: the devil (whether directly or
through the religious authorities) may be 'testing' or 'tempting'
Jesus, but in effect his temptation amounts to the suggestion
that it is God himself who needs to be tested.[57]

Before we leave this group of signs which Jesus *refused* to do,
we must consider two passages from the Fourth Gospel that are
relevant to our theme. In John 2.13–22, we find John's version
of the story of the disturbance in the temple, which the other
evangelists place at the end of their narratives. The reaction of
Jesus' opponents to the havoc he has caused is to demand 'What
sign can you show us for doing this?' – in other words, 'What
sign can you show us to prove your credentials for behaving in
this way?' The Synoptics record a similar reaction from the
religious authorities after this incident, but in their accounts this
takes the form of questions: 'By what authority are you doing
these things? Who gave you this authority?'[58] Jesus' reply, as we
have noted, is to appeal to the baptism of John. The sign
demanded in the Fourth Gospel is an authenticating miracle, as
in the Synoptic stories we have been examining in this chapter,
though the demand here follows, not a miracle, but an incident
which John, at least, clearly regards as a prophetic action. Jesus'

answer is remarkably similar to his answer to the demand for a sign in the Synoptics, though in John he directs his opponents, not to the sign of Jonah, but to the significance of the sign he himself has just performed. As in Matt. 12.40, this sign is interpreted as a reference to the resurrection.

The second demand for a sign in John occurs at 6.30, where the crowd ask Jesus, 'What sign are you going to do, so that we may see it and believe in you?' They then apparently suggest the sign they wish to see – 'Our fathers ate manna in the wilderness, as it is written, "He gave them bread to eat from heaven."' The demand is an extraordinary one, in view of the fact that John has described the same crowd (which had followed Jesus because of the signs he had performed, 6.2) as having been fed by Jesus in a miraculous fashion on the previous day. One can, of course, argue that John has combined two sources, and that he has done it badly, but he, at least, seems to believe that the crowd that demands a sign in v.30 is the same crowd that has just witnessed one – and even more absurd, is now demanding to see precisely the sign that Jesus has already performed! The very absurdity of their demand points to the explanation. To the evangelist at least the point is that though at one level the crowd witnesses what Jesus does, it nevertheless completely fails to see the *significance* of what Jesus is doing. Those who demand a sign have clearly failed to recognize the sign that has been given – have failed to see that the bread which Jesus gave them is the manna that they ask for, and that it signifies the living bread which is Jesus himself.

Although both these passages obviously reflect Johannine interpretation, the way in which Jesus is said in both of them to refuse to give a sign of the kind which is being demanded, and to point instead to the true significance of what he has already done, is consistent with the Synoptic tradition. Jesus is presented in all the Gospels as one who refused to perform authenticating miracles. The true prophetic signs (whether performed by himself or by John) pointed to the *significance* of what he was doing, and not simply to his miraculous powers.

Jesus refuses to perform authenticating miracles. But on one occasion he is recorded as having performed a miracle in order to demonstrate his authority to forgive sins. All three Synoptic evangelists record the story of the paralytic in the same form: Jesus first told the man that his sins were forgiven; the religious authorities were outraged at his words, whereupon he healed the man – in order, it is said, that his accusers might know 'that the Son of man has authority on earth to forgive sins'.[59] This, together with the account of Jesus' message to John,[60] is the closest the Synoptic evangelists come to offering us a *sēmeion* in the sense of an 'authenticating miracle' or 'proof'. How, then, does it come about that Jesus is here said to have *offered* a sign of his authority, not, this time, to enquirers anxious to believe, but to opponents, without even being required to do so? Interestingly, it is not *described* as a *sēmeion*. When we examine the story more closely, moreover, we realize that Jesus' action is not an 'authenticating miracle' (of the somewhat tangential kind performed by Moses) intended to prove that he is a true prophet, but rather a *prophetic* sign which demonstrates the much more significant thing that the Son of man has *already* done.[61] Although the healing is said to have been done in response to a challenge from Jesus' opponents, it is far more than a 'proof' of Jesus' power. The prophetic drama which is enacted – Jesus healing a paralysed man, who gets up, picks up his bed and walks out – is a sign that his sins have indeed been forgiven: the liberation which we *see* is an indication of a far more important liberation which we cannot observe.

To understand this story fully, however, we have to consider it in the context of Jesus' other prophetic actions, and to these we now turn.

III

'The Signs of a Prophet'

Jesus refuses to perform authenticating miracles. The miracles he *is* said to perform are not intended as mere 'proofs' of his authority to do what he is doing, but are themselves significant actions which effect God's saving purpose. Many of these miracles, to be sure, have often been interpreted by later Christian thinkers as though their purpose was to provide 'proofs' of Jesus' identity as Messiah and Son of God. Indeed, one can see this tendency at work already in the Gospels: thus the Matthaean account of the walking on the water leads up to the confession that Jesus is the Son of God.[1] This particular miracle fits uneasily into the Synoptic narrative, since it seems to have no purpose – unless it be to reveal Jesus' identity. Yet even this story is told by the evangelists not, as we shall see, to *authenticate* Jesus' power, but rather to reveal what it is that is taking place in him.

1. Miracles

The story of the walking on the water raises problems of another kind: can it tell us anything at all about what Jesus himself did? This particular narrative is one of the clearest examples of the difficulty of accepting the miracle stories at the historical level: certainly it cannot be regarded as contradicting the clear evidence we examined in the last chapter that Jesus refused to perform signs. But the story reminds us that any discussion of miracles is bound to raise difficult problems of historicity: what kind of credence can we give to these stories? We cannot embark on a discussion of the huge topic of historicity here, and

fortunately there is no need. For our purposes it is sufficient to
note that, whatever attitude we may take to the so-called
'nature miracles', there is sufficient evidence in the tradition to
argue that Jesus must have carried out *some* healings and
exorcisms. I notice that E. P. Sanders includes Jesus' healing
activity in his list of 'almost indisputable facts' about Jesus.[2]
And because he was known as a healer and exorcist, Jesus was
recognized also as a prophet: such activity would have identified
him as a prophetic, rather than as a messianic, figure. The
stories told about him, whatever their historical basis, therefore
represent him as a prophet. Whether we treat them as fundamentally historical or as later creations of the community, these
stories confirm that Jesus was seen as a prophet, whose actions
were understood as manifestations of divine power.

Almost all of the miracles attributed to Jesus are understood
by our evangelists, then, as manifestations of divine power. All
the healing miracles fall into this category, since they are seen
as examples of God's saving power at work – an idea which
is sometimes underlined when Jesus says 'Your faith has
saved you'. The exorcisms of unclean spirits and restorations
to life and health indicate that God's salvation is bursting
into the world. The stories of Jesus feeding vast crowds are also
presented by the evangelists as epiphanies – manifestations of
divine power; moreover, they remind us of the Exodus, for they
evoke memories of how Israel was fed in the desert. In the same
way, the accounts of Jesus' ability to still the storm and walk on
water recall God's control of the elements and Israel's escape
through the Red Sea. These miracles are similar to the first
group of prophetic actions referred to in Chapter I, which were
all direct manifestations of divine power. They are clearly seen
by the evangelists as indications that God is at work in Jesus.

These many and various stories of miracles – accounts of
Jesus healing men and women and exorcizing demons, feeding
the crowds and controlling the elements – can also be seen,
however, as prophetic dramas. For as well as being present
manifestations of God's power, they point to something which
is as yet hidden but which is certainly going to happen – which,

indeed, has already begun to happen. Healing miracles in themselves reveal God's life-giving power, but Jesus' message to John
reminds us that they are pointers to the fact that Jesus is the One
whose coming heralds salvation.[3] Elsewhere he argues that his
exorcisms are a sign that the Kingdom of God is bursting into
this world, and that Satan's kingdom is crumbling.[4] If, by the
finger – or Spirit – of God, he is casting out demons, then the
Kingdom has already arrived: the drama of the exorcisms
points to the hidden reality of Satan's defeat. It is immediately
after this that he goes on to talk about the sign of Jonah, and
the judgment of the generation which fails to repent.[5] The
stories about Jesus feeding the crowd and controlling the sea
demonstrate that God is about to save his people by means of
an even greater Exodus than he achieved through Moses. All the
miracles, therefore, can be seen as pointing beyond themselves:
they are *signs* as well as *wonders*.

An interesting confirmation of this is found in the story of the
healing of the Syro-Phoenician woman's daughter, told by both
Matthew and Mark.[6] To modern readers, the surprising thing
about this narrative is Jesus' reluctance to heal the child: in both
accounts, he brushes her mother's request aside quite brusquely,
telling her that the bread intended for the children must not be
thrown to the dogs. Nevertheless, when she persists he grants
her request. Commentators have been hard pressed to explain
Jesus' attitude, but if we remember the link between Jesus'
proclamation of the Kingdom and his healing miracles the
explanation is clear. Jesus' healings are part of the inbreaking of
the Kingdom, and healings can therefore take place only where
people respond to him in faith.[7] But this woman has by her per-
sistence demonstrated her faith. Had Jesus healed a Jewish
child, that would certainly have been a prophetic sign, since it
would have pointed to the fact that the salvation of God's
people was imminent. If a *Gentile* child is now healed, this is a
prophetic sign of something even more significant – namely,
that God's salvation is already reaching out to the Gentiles, and
that the good news will, in time, be taken to them.

Another Synoptic story about the healing of a Gentile makes

a similar point. The centurion whose servant is healed shows extraordinary faith – far greater than that shown by Jesus' own countrymen.[8] The significance of the healing is seen in the comment added in Matthew: 'I tell you, many will come from east and west and will eat with Abraham and Isaac and Jacob in the Kingdom of heaven.' The servant's cure is the prophetic sign of the salvation that is to come to the Gentiles. It is no surprise to find that both of these stories record that the healing was performed at a distance – an indication that Jesus has not yet proclaimed the gospel to the Gentiles, since his mission is to Israel alone; this is specifically said in Matt. 15.24, and implied in Luke's arrangement of the material, since he reserves the Gentile mission for his second volume.

The third example of a Gentile healing is very different.[9] It is not even clear that the Gerasene demoniac *is* a Gentile – though the fact that he is living in Gentile territory suggests that he is. The unclean spirits who possess him cause him to live in an unclean place, and when Jesus drives them out, they transfer to a herd of unclean pigs. Their instinct for self-destruction, already seen in the behaviour of the demoniac, reaches a climax in the death of the pigs, which is presumably understood to entail the destruction of the demons as well: Satan's kingdom is crumbling before Jesus' authority. Very unusually, the restored man is told to go and *tell* his own people what the Lord has done for him. Is this, too, a sign that though Jesus does not preach to the Gentiles, others will be entrusted with the task of proclaiming the good news to them?

2. *Other prophetic actions*

Let us turn now to those other actions of Jesus which (though not miraculous) clearly have special significance, and can be considered as examples of prophetic signs or dramas, remembering what it is that we are meaning by the term 'prophetic sign': *not* a visual aid intended to *assist* in teaching – rather, the dramatic *equivalent* of the spoken oracle; *not* an efficacious act, which *causes* something to happen – rather, the dramatic *embodiment* of the divine purpose, which otherwise may well be at present hidden.

Some of these actions are incidents with which we are so familiar that we are accustomed to thinking of them as simply 'part of the story'. Like some of the examples of prophetic drama performed by the Old Testament prophets, their significance often passes us by, because they seem so ordinary. Jesus' choice of twelve disciples is clearly significant – as is his sending out of these Twelve on a mission to Israel. The existence of the Twelve is another of the items included, after some hesitation, among Sanders' '(almost) indisputable facts about Jesus'.[10] The various lists of disciples who were believed to be among the Twelve do not tally – but the idea that there were twelve is embedded in the tradition. The number clearly symbolizes the twelve tribes of Israel, and the existence of this group, as Jeremias long ago argued, 'announces the establishment of the eschatological people of God'.[11] In other words, the choice of twelve men was a prophetic sign: the fact that they had been called together by Jesus was a sign that the scattered tribes of Israel would be gathered together by God. It is not just that the Twelve 'represent' gathered Israel: rather, by appointing the Twelve to be with him and to share his mission, Jesus expresses in dramatic form God's intention for Israel, the fulfilment of which still lies in the future, but which is nevertheless certain. That intention is confirmed in Jesus' promise to his disciples that they will have a share in his Kingdom and sit on thrones, exercising rule over the twelve tribes of Israel.[12]

All four Gospels record the tradition that Jesus renamed Simon, one of his disciples, giving him the name 'Peter' or 'Cephas'.[13] A name meaning 'rock' seems a highly inappropriate nickname for someone with Peter's character, and the name could hardly be a description of what he was like; it was clearly intended to be a prophetic sign – an indication of the role Peter was going to play in the new community.[14] This renaming reminds us of the way in which Hosea and Isaiah deliberately gave prophetic names to some of their children.[15]

Jesus' action in eating with tax-collectors and sinners was

another prophetic sign – a dramatic indication of the nature of God's forgiveness, and of the people whom God was calling into his Kingdom. When Jesus outrages the religious authorities by dining with outsiders, the meal is a foretaste of the messianic banquet, and a symbol of those who will be invited to the feast – and of those who will be excluded. This is hinted at in his concluding words, 'I came not to invite the righteous but sinners'; the feast to which they are invited is not simply an earthly one.[16] When Jesus chooses to spend the day with Zacchaeus, and calls him down from the tree, that is a prophetic drama which represents God's purpose to save the lost.[17] Zacchaeus' immediate repentance confirms the truth of the sign, and reveals Zacchaeus to be a son of Abraham, who will share in the blessings of Israel.

Keeping dubious company is not the only action on Jesus' part which is said to have caused outrage. The story of the healing of the paralytic, which I have already discussed, is another such incident. For the evangelists, this is a clear prophetic drama – Jesus' healing of a paralysed man, who gets up, picks up his bed and walks out, is interpreted as a sign that in the ministry of Jesus, men and women are experiencing the forgiveness of their sins.

On three occasions, it is the actions of Jesus' *disciples*, rather than his own, which cause offence. On one of these, he is questioned about their failure to fast;[18] on another, he is asked why they are doing something which breaks the sabbath laws;[19] and on a third they are accused of doing something which is contrary to the traditions of the elders.[20] These incidents are hardly prophetic dramas, since they are not initiated by Jesus himself. But Jesus is regarded as responsible for his disciples' actions, and is said to have justified them. Moreover, Old Testament prophets sometimes involved other people in their dramatic acts.[21] And by their handling of the traditions, the evangelists in effect *treat* these incidents as prophetic signs. The failure of the disciples to fast is seen as a sign that the bridegroom is present; the plucking and eating of grain is interpreted as a dramatic representation of the authority of the Son of man over the sabbath; and the fact that they eat with unwashed hands is interpreted by a 'parable' to the effect that it is not what enters a person that defiles him, but what comes out.

Such scandalous behaviour on the part of Jesus and his disciples is thus an integral part of his message: just as his parables proclaim the coming of God's Kingdom, and portray the character of God's forgiving grace, so Jesus' actions, and those of his disciples, offer dramatic demonstrations of the joys of the future Kingdom, which is already bursting in.

There is one further action by the disciples – this time at Jesus' express command – which leads to a final interpretative comment by Jesus, and which is an example of a prophetic drama. This is the story of the large draught of fish, recorded in Luke 5.1–11. Only the Fourth Gospel relates a similar narrative, and there it is a resurrection story.[22] Once again, this story raises historical problems: was it a miracle? Where does it belong in the narrative? But let us concentrate on looking at the story in the form in which Luke gives it. Jesus instructs Simon (who has been fishing all night to no avail) to sail out into the deep water of the lake and let down his nets. When he does so, he has to summon James and John to help with the huge catch of fish. Jesus then tells Simon: 'Do not fear; from now on you will catch people.' In this form, the story is a clear prophetic drama: the catching of fish at Jesus' command is a sure sign of what the disciples are going to do as his followers.

But the disciples were going to meet resistance as well as response in the course of their mission, and when Jesus sent them out, two by two, to proclaim the good news, he is said to have commanded them to shake the dust from their feet on leaving those who refused to receive them: the dramatic action is an obvious symbol of rejection.[23]

All three of our Synoptic evangelists record an incident in which a dispute among the disciples regarding their status leads Jesus to respond to the argument by calling a child to join the group, and then using the child to drive home the point of his teaching.[24] Unfortunately, however, the evangelists disagree as to which sayings belong at this point. The most straightforward account is found in Matthew 18, where Jesus says 'Unless you

turn and become like children, you will never enter the Kingdom of heaven; whoever humbles himself like this child will be
great in the Kingdom of heaven.' This makes good sense: the
disciples have been trying to establish their own importance,
and are reminded that this desire for status is totally contrary to
the rules that appply to God's Kingdom. They must humble
themselves, and become like children, who make no pretensions
to status. Jesus then continues: 'And whoever receives one such
child in my name receives me.' In this context these words are
perhaps intended to remind us that Jesus is himself the one who
is truly humble, and therefore like a child; thus to receive a child
in Jesus' name is to receive Jesus himself. In Matthew's version
therefore, the child, who has no claims or pretensions to status,
symbolizes the attitude that men and women need to show if
they are to enter God's Kingdom.

The version in Mark 9 and Luke 9 is somewhat different.
Both evangelists omit the saying about becoming like a child at
this point, and use it in the story of Jesus *blessing* the children,
where it seems far less appropriate.[25] In their version of the
dispute, Jesus' action in summoning the child is followed
immediately by the saying about receiving a child being the
equivalent of receiving Jesus. This seems to make little sense on
its own. Both evangelists include a saying about greatness,
however: Luke ends the pericope with the saying 'the least
among you all is the greatest', while in Mark, the saying
precedes Jesus' action, and runs as follows: 'If anyone would be
first, let him be last of all, and servant of all.' Matthew Black
long ago suggested that what we have here is an acted parable,
playing on the double meaning of the Aramaic word *talya*,
which means both 'child' and 'servant'.[26] The child set in the
midst of the disciples is thus the dramatic representation of the
servant whom the disciple is required to become. Although the
evangelists have used different traditions of this story, all of
them see the child as a symbol of true discipleship.

In none of its versions, however, is this story a true prophetic
drama. Jesus uses the child to demonstrate the point that he is
trying to convey to his disciples: his action signifies, not what

will be, but what *should* be. The story is thus an example of an acted parable, not a prophetic drama: it is useful to us, precisely because it reminds us of the difference.

3. Jerusalem

Let us turn now to the group of prophetic signs associated with Jerusalem. First, there is the story found in all four Gospels of Jesus' entry into Jerusalem.[27] The fact that the Synoptic evangelists all describe the special arrangements made by Jesus in order to procure the donkey underlines their conviction that *riding* into the city was a deliberate action on his part. But what did that action signify? The united testimony of the four evangelists that Jesus – after trudging so many miles on foot! – rode this final stage of the journey is remarkable, and indicates that we are here on firm historical ground, since pilgrims normally all entered Jerusalem on foot. Far from being the act of humility which Christian tradition has made it, this was an extraordinarily bold and ostentatious gesture.[28] The insistence of Mark and Luke that the animal had never been ridden before suggests that it was therefore fit to be ridden by a king or for some sacred purpose. In Matthew and Mark, the entry follows immediately after an incident in which Jesus has been hailed as 'Son of David' as he leaves Jericho *en route* for Jerusalem, and we are reminded of the incident in I Kings 1.32–40 when David, on his deathbed, commanded the priest Zadok and the prophet Nathan to mount Solomon on David's own mule, escort him to Gihon, anoint him king and bring him back to Jerusalem to the acclamation of the people.[29] The evangelists certainly saw the messianic implications of their story: Mark simply hints at this by saying that the crowd hailed 'the coming kingdom of our father David', but in Matthew, Jesus is hailed as Son of David, and in Luke and John he is welcomed as king; Matthew and John refer specifically to Zech. 9.9; the Synoptic evangelists all describe how people spread greenery or garments on the road. Jesus himself offers no explanation, but the evangelists are surely right in their interpretation: to enter

Jerusalem on the back of an ass, instead of on foot, was to make a messianic claim.[30] We have here another clear example of a prophetic drama: if God's anointed one is entering Jerusalem, this is a sign that God's Kingdom will surely come in power.

According to the Synoptics, Jesus' first act on arriving in Jerusalem was to enter the temple. In Matthew and Luke he immediately drove out those who were selling goods there. Matthew's account is somewhat more detailed than Luke's, and so is that given by Mark, who has intercalated this story with that of the barren fig tree. By doing so, he has made it clear that he has understood Jesus' action in the temple as a prophetic sign of its coming destruction.

Let us therefore look first at this story of the barren fig tree.[31] It is found only in Matthew and Mark, but Luke records a parable that is similar – though in the parable the gardener pleads with the tree's owner to allow it one more year to produce fruit before it is cut down.[32] The parable is clearly a warning of the destruction which awaits those who do not repent and bear fruit in their lives. The story in Matthew and Mark raises problems because of its miraculous element; it is possible that originally it was an acted parable in which Jesus denounced a barren tree. Whatever its origins, as it stands in Matthew and Mark the story is an example of a prophetic drama: Jesus looked for fruit on a fig tree – a tree which, incidentally, was very likely a recognized symbol for Israel; a tree which should have been bearing fruit because the messianic era was dawning (even though, according to Mark, it was not the *season* for figs).[33] But the tree was barren, and Jesus pronounced a curse on it. The drama symbolizes Israel's failure to respond to her Messiah and the inevitable destruction to which that failure will lead.

All the Gospels record the story of Jesus' actions in the temple,[34] and all of them contain hints that the incident was seen by the evangelists as a sign of the temple's future destruction. These hints are found chiefly in the context of the story. Mark, as we have already noted, intercalates the story with that of the fig tree; Matthew places the two stories in close proximity, and

backs them both up with three parables about Israel's failure –
the parables of the two sons, the vineyard, and the wedding
banquet.[35] In Luke, the incident in the temple follows the
account of how Jesus wept over the city because it was to be
razed to the ground.[36] In John, Jesus himself is said to have
followed up his action with the words: 'Destroy this temple, and
in three days I will raise it up.'[37] With Sanders, we can surely
assume that 'it is overwhelmingly probable that Jesus did *something* in the temple.'[38] But was the incident intended *by Jesus* to
be a sign of the temple's coming destruction? Or was it what it
has traditionally been interpreted as being, a 'cleansing' of the
temple? Should his actions be seen primarily as a *protest*, rather
than as a prophecy of the temple's fate? Sanders denies that
what Jesus did is to be seen as a cleansing, arguing that the provision of suitable animals for sacrifice and of coinage for the
temple tax was a necessary part of temple worship and would
not have seemed corrupt at the time.[39] He interprets Jesus'
action as a prophetic sign 'that the end was at hand and that the
temple would be destroyed, so that the new and perfect temple
might arise'.[40] But *why* would the temple be destroyed? Was it,
as Sanders suggests, simply in order that a new one might be
built, because that was part of the eschatological programme?
Or was it because God had judged his people and found them
guilty? I have argued elsewhere[41] that though Sanders may be
right in maintaining that Jesus did not condemn temple
sacrifices in themselves, he is wrong in ignoring the notion of
judgment implicit in the events in the temple. Certainly the
evangelists believed that Jesus condemned those who failed to
produce ethical fruit.[42] His teaching in the temple affirms that
love for God and neighbour are the central commandment,[43]
and he condemned the scribes for their hypocrisy and their
oppression of others.[44] The parables make clear that the nation
was under judgment because of her failure to respond to Jesus'
message. So does his lament over Jerusalem.[45] Jesus followed
in the tradition of the prophets, who foretold the destruction
of Jerusalem and the temple because of the failure of its
inhabitants to respond to God.[46]

I have long assumed that the evangelists were basically right in their interpretation of the incident as a sign of its future destruction, though I have argued in the past that Jesus' action was intended as a *warning* of what would happen if the worshippers did not repent, rather than as a sign of certain destruction.[47] In other words, Jesus was not only protesting about what was taking place in the temple, but demonstrating what divine judgment on the people would mean. By the time the Gospels were written, however, the temple had probably already been destroyed, and it is hardly surprising if the Synoptic evangelists interpreted the sign as meaning that destruction was inevitable. In the context in which they have placed the incident, during the last week of Jesus' life, that interpretation seems obvious. But it is possible that when Jesus caused havoc in the temple he was still hoping for repentance, and if John is right, and this incident took place earlier in the ministry, his action might well have been intended as a warning.[48]

But it has to be admitted that Jesus' action is by no means an obvious symbol of coming destruction: Jeremiah's breaking of the jar was a far more appropriate way to express that. What in fact Jesus is said by all four evangelists to have done was to interrupt the financial dealings in the temple – the changing of money, the buying and selling of animals for sacrifice; in the Fourth Gospel, Jesus specifically complains that the traders have turned the temple into a market.[49] Mark adds that he prevented people using the temple as a short-cut, a practice which was forbidden in the Mishnah[50] because it implied disrespect. We do not have to suppose that financial dealings in the temple were corrupt in order to believe that Jesus' protest was based on a conviction that many of those who worshipped there were failing to love God with heart and soul and mind and strength, and that the worship they offered was therefore hollow. It was Mark, again, who made the point clear by reminding us that such love is far greater than all burnt offerings and sacrifice,[51] and he may well have had the words of I Sam. 15.22 in mind:

Has the Lord as great delight in burnt offerings and sacrifices
as in obeying the voice of the Lord?

The evangelists understood Jesus' action as pointing to the
temple's destruction. But have they in fact interpreted the drama
correctly? Or was it originally directed at the worship taking
place in the temple, rather than at the temple itself? Looked at
in isolation from the *setting* the evangelists have given it, and
leaving aside John's interpretation in 2.18–22, the story itself
suggests a protest about what is going on in the temple. Let us
suppose for a moment that *Amos* had delivered *his* message
about the temple in the form of a prophetic drama instead of an
oracle. What would he have done to convey the burden of the
following words?[52]

I hate, I despise your festivals,
  and I take no delight in your solemn assemblies.
Even though you offer me your burnt offerings and grain
  offerings,
I will not accept them;
  and the peace offerings of your fatted animals
I will not accept . . .
But let justice roll down like waters,
  and righteousness like an everflowing stream.

Was Jesus' action perhaps intended as *a prophetic drama
signifying God's rejection of the worship taking place in
the temple*? And was that worship inadequate because the
worshippers were failing to obey God in their lives? The words
attributed to Jesus by all three Synoptic evangelists – 'It is
written "My house shall be called a house of prayer", but you
have made it a den of thieves' – certainly fit that interpretation.[53]
The traders are condemned, not because their practices are
necessarily corrupt (though they may have been), but because
they were more interested in their trade and their profits than in
the worship of God. If that was the original meaning of Jesus'
action, it would correspond to his protest about the fig tree
which failed to bear fruit, and to the parable about the vineyard

tenants who failed to pay the owner what was due to him. The evangelists, however, see the story in a different light – not surprisingly if, as seems probable, they are writing in the light of the events of AD 70. It is the *context* they have given to the incident that makes this prophetic drama point to a future event which will cause worship to cease altogether.

4. *The Last Supper*

And so we come to the climax of the story, and to the final example of prophetic drama in the Synoptics. Jesus took bread, and after saying the blessing, broke it and shared it among his disciples with the words 'This is my body'; after supper, we are told, he took a cup and gave it to them, once again with an explanatory sentence, whose wording differs in the various accounts. This is the one Gospel story that my husband discussed in any detail – and he was hoping to write a book about it: it is clearly impossible to explore it in depth here. But let us at least consider briefly how it functions as prophetic drama.

Jesus' actions at the Last Supper are frequently interpreted as 'prophetic signs', and they fall readily into that category.[54] The prophets often used material objects, as Jesus does here, and they 'identified' them with something else – as Jeremiah, for example, did with his earthenware jar.[55] In Jeremiah's case, his action in breaking the jar was, as we have already noted, a clear symbol of coming destruction. But what of Jesus' action in breaking the bread? Was *that* a sign of destruction? Or is this an interpretation which becomes clear, as in the case of his action in the temple, *after* the event? The scribe who added the participle *klōmenon*, meaning 'broken', to Paul's account of the story in I Cor.11.24 tried to make the link between the breaking of the bread and the death of Jesus explicit, but it has to be said that the symbolism is by no means obvious: it is only centuries of Christian interpretation that make it seem so. When you smash a jar into pieces you destroy it, but when you break bread you *share* it – and that is what Jesus does here: he gives the bread to his disciples so that they can eat it. All our sources agree that in doing so, he said 'This is my body'. Again, we misunderstand what is happening because we interpret the word 'body', *sōma*, as meaning 'flesh'. But in its Jewish context, the word represented by *sōma* must surely have meant 'self'.[56] In other words, Jesus was saying 'This is myself – this is me'. My husband was intrigued by an idea of Robert Eisler, taken up by David Daube[57] and recently developed by Deborah Carmichael,[58] that to understand Jesus' action we need to look at the *afikoman*, the name given to a piece of unleavened bread which is broken off the loaf and put aside at the beginning of the Passover meal,[59] and then shared at the end. No one is clear as to the origin of this ritual, but Daube took the word *afikoman* to have been derived from the Greek *aphikomenos*, meaning 'He who comes'. The loaf, he argued, was understood to represent the people of Israel, and the fragment broken off stood for the Messiah. This suggestion, if it is correct, helps us to understand how Jesus might have understood the loaf to represent himself, and both Daube and Carmichael interpret the action as a self-revelation by Jesus to his disciples, identifying himself with the Messiah. But this does not really explain what Jesus *did* at the Last Supper, for he *broke* the bread and passed it round – that is, he *shared* it among his disciples. It is this action which is important, and its importance is evidenced by subsequent references to the breaking of bread: the risen Lord is known to two disciples in the breaking of bread;[60] the disciples are said to meet together to break bread;[61] and Paul refers to the bread at the eucharist as 'the bread which we break'.[62] When Jesus broke the bread in the upper room, the action was a significant one; but what did it mean?

My husband's suggestion was that Jesus took over an everyday action – breaking and sharing bread – an action which would in itself have conveyed the idea of fellowship, and gave it a special meaning: when he broke and shared the loaf among his disciples, in a way which was clearly memorable, this was an action which, like all prophetic dramas, had significance on a grand scale. By this action, Jesus represented the divine activity which was at work, creating and bonding a new community.

The bread was divided among many, but the one loaf signified that there was to be one community. This community was not just a group of like-minded men and women, but those to whom Jesus had as it were made himself over, those who were entrusted with the task of continuing his existence and activity after his death. In some ways, the action is like that of Elijah, casting his cloak over Elisha,[63] but Jesus' action symbolizes not a mere succession, but the creation of a new community – or rather, the recreation of Israel: all the accounts of the Last Supper stress the presence of the Twelve, the symbol of Israel.[64] Jesus' words are not primarily a comment on the atoning significance of his death; rather they point to the significance of what God was doing as a *result* of his death. The sharing of the bread represents the birth of the church. The tradition emphasizes this element of sharing: they share one loaf, eat from a common dish,[65] and drink from a common cup.[66]

There is confirmation of this interpretation in the reference to the Lord's Supper in I Cor. 10.16f., where Paul explains what the breaking of the bread signifies: it is a *koinōnia (a common sharing)* in the body of Christ. The point is clearly important, for he spells it out: 'because there is one loaf, *we who are many are one body, for we all share in the one loaf*'. This explanation is the more remarkable, since Paul is not concerned in this passage to stress the unity of the Christian community (a theme which he takes up in his discussion of the Lord's Supper in I Corinthians 11, and in his exposition of the analogy of the body in I Corinthians 12): rather is he concerned to emphasize that it is impossible to partake of both the Lord's table and the table of demons.[67] Paul here spells out the fact that by *sharing* in the bread, many individuals are made one community – a community which can be described as 'one body'. Was this, as has been suggested,[68] the origin of Paul's understanding of the church as the body *of Christ*? It is often objected[69] that there is a great gap between *eating* the bread called 'the body of Christ' and *becoming* the body of Christ, but this is to ignore the fact that the bread is *shared* before it is *eaten*. If it was Jesus' action in *sharing* the bread which signified the creation of a community that was to continue his life and work, Paul's use of the phrase 'the body of Christ' for the community is explicable and apt. The church is the body of Christ because the bread which its members break and share is a common sharing in the body of Christ.

Is this what Paul is referring to when he speaks in I Cor. 11.29 about those who fail to 'discern the body'? Certainly the words occur in a context where Paul is complaining about the schisms in the Corinthian community, which are apparent even at the Lord's Supper. It is possible that Paul is playing on the double significance of the word *sōma*: anyone who eats the bread and drinks the cup unworthily will be guilty of the body and blood of the Lord; but he will also eat and drink judgment on himself if he fails to discern the *sōma* – the common fellowship of the whole Christian community.

For Paul, the cup of wine – 'the cup of blessing, which we bless' – is also a *koinōnia*, a common sharing in the blood of Christ (I Cor. 10.16). But what of the wine at the Last Supper itself? The evidence here is by no means as clear, and my husband was inclined to believe that the traditions about the wine did not in fact go back to the upper room. But the fact that all our traditions (including the reference in I Cor. 10.16f.) say *something* about the cup suggests that it was part of the original story, however overlaid with different interpretations it has become. Again, they all refer to the *cup*, not to the wine itself, thus emphasizing the fact that the wine, too, was shared. In Luke, the 'first' cup is given to the disciples with the specific command, 'Take this and share it among yourselves'.[70] One interesting feature of the Synoptic accounts of the cup is that they all link it with a future ratification in the Kingdom of God. In both Mark and Matthew, the story ends with Jesus' words: 'Truly I tell you, I will not drink of the fruit of the vine again, until I drink it new in the Kingdom of God.'[71] In Luke, these words follow the drinking of the cup at the *beginning* of the meal, and they follow a parallel saying about not eating the passover until it is fulfilled in the Kingdom of God.[72] If we accept the shorter text of Luke (omitting vv.19b–20), as I in any case would wish to do, the whole emphasis of his narrative is on this idea of future fulfilment in the Kingdom of God. Addressing his disciples a little later in Luke's account, Jesus says: 'I covenant to you a kingdom, even as my Father covenanted to me, so that you may eat and drink at my table in my kingdom.'[73] If Jesus passed a cup of wine round his disciples, this was surely another prophetic action. Were they, in drinking the wine, enacting *the future coming of God's Kingdom and the messianic banquet*? Wine plays a significant part in Jewish descriptions of future blessing,[74] and will thus be drunk at the messianic banquet. Bread and wine are specifically mentioned in I QSa 2, in the description of the community meal in the last days, when the two Messiahs are present.[75] Paul, too, has this forward-looking element, even though for him the emphasis is now on Christ's death. He ends his account of the Last Supper in I Cor. 11.23–26 with the words: 'For as often as you eat this bread and drink the cup you *proclaim* the Lord's death *until he comes*.' The ritual based on the original story – the celebration of the eucharist – has now itself become a drama enacted by the community – a drama which proclaims Christ's death until he comes.

All our traditions (apart from the shorter text of Luke) now link the wine with Jesus' blood, and thus specifically with his death; but all of them interpret this also as the blood *of the covenant*, poured out for many (or, in Luke, for 'you').[76] Once again, we have here the notion that God is creating a new community. The brief reference in I Cor. 10.16 speaks simply of the cup of blessing being a common sharing in the blood of Christ; but the idea of the new community is, as we have already seen, stressed in v.17. In the account of the sealing of the covenant between God and his people in Exodus 24, Moses is said to have thrown the blood of the covenant on the people.[77] The offering of wine by Jesus to his disciples is now seen by the evangelists as another dramatic action, representing the reality of the new covenant being established by God through Jesus' death: the wine poured into the cup points to the life[78] of Jesus poured out in death. But the wine is *drunk* – an anomaly when it is compared with blood. In so far as the wine represents blood, it cannot be drunk.[79] However, the idea that two parties can enter into a covenant by eating and drinking together is not an unusual one.[80] The sharing of the disciples in the cup indicates that they all share in the covenant which God now makes with his people, and in the new life which that covenant brings. The drinking, like the eating, means that the disciples are members of the covenant community and will share in the messianic banquet. The idea of the covenant thus holds together two ideas (the pouring out of blood and the drinking of the cup) which would otherwise be incompatible.

It is possible, then, that two ideas have coalesced in the traditions about the Last Supper. One is wine which is drunk in expectation of the messianic feast; the other is blood poured out in death, sealing the new covenant. These two ideas have been brought together, and the wine which is drunk has been merged with the wine which (representing shed blood) is poured out; the resultant saying over the cup has then been conformed to that over the bread. There is evidence for this process in Luke, where (in the longer text) we have two cups, the first of which is linked with the idea of eating and drinking in the Kingdom of God (a theme found in all our traditions), while the second is the cup which is poured out as 'the new covenant in my blood'. Are these perhaps different traditions about the same cup? Is it perhaps the first cup – a firm part of the Lucan tradition whichever text we accept – that represents the earlier tradition about the cup of wine? And does the alternative saying, which made its way into Christian liturgy, represent the interpretation given when the saying over the wine was assimilated to that over the bread?

Scholarly attention has almost always been focussed on the significance of the elements of bread and wine themselves, and on the words which Jesus is said to have spoken over them. It is certainly time to consider whether his actions are not at least as important as his words and as the elements he used. It was what Jesus *did* with the bread and the wine that became the basis of the church's rite, as we are reminded by the specific command to 'do this' in Paul and Luke. Both the breaking of the bread and the offering of the wine are, I suggest, to be understood as prophetic actions pointing to the significance of what is taking place in and through the death of Jesus.

These traditions of the Last Supper complete the Synoptic record of Jesus' dramatic actions. The Fourth Gospel, of course, has a very different account of this final meal. But we must save that for discussion in the final chapter on the interpretation of Jesus' prophetic actions by the evangelists.

IV

'More than a Prophet'

We turn now to the different ways in which the four evangelists interpreted Jesus' prophetic actions. Needless to say, the evidence we have already examined also bore the stamp of their interpretation, but our concern now is to look at the particular way in which each individual author handled his material.[1]

1. Mark

We begin with Mark, since I am still persuaded that Markan priority is the most likely hypothesis to explain our Gospels' origins. It is noteworthy that almost all the miracles recorded by Mark occur in the first half of the Gospel. He has surely arranged them in this way not, as some have suggested, to present us with a false christology,[2] but to persuade us that Jesus is superior to the prophets who have gone before him. Mark tells us first of Jesus' authoritative actions, including many miracles, then raises the question of the source of his authority: in a dispute with the scribes, Jesus affirms that he is acting in the power of the Holy Spirit and not Beelzebul. At the very least, therefore, we know that he must be a true prophet, not a false one. There follows a series of even more remarkable miracles, all of which are reminiscent of the miracles performed by Moses, but which are interpreted as greater than those he did. Jesus' actions go beyond the actions which might be expected of a prophet, and therefore pose the question 'Who can this be, since even the wind and sea obey him?'[3] Already we are being made to think of Jesus as greater than a prophet. Twice we are told that popular opinion is that he is a prophet of some kind, but at Caesarea Philippi Peter stumbles on part of the truth when he acknowledges him as the Messiah. These 'prophetic' actions of Jesus are interpreted by Mark, then, not simply as dramatic signs that the Kingdom of God is bursting in, nor simply as manifestations of divine power, but – paradoxically – as manifestations of Jesus' own superiority to the prophets.

It is because the miracles tell us who Jesus is that the opening of blind eyes is so significant, and why accounts of the healing of blind men are placed at strategic points in Mark's narrative.[4] Only those whose eyes are opened are able to see the truth about Jesus; only those whose ears are unstopped can hear the good news and proclaim it.[5] During his ministry, men and women's eyes and ears remained closed to the truth, but these miracles are dramatic signs of what *will* happen after the resurrection. In the story of the Transfiguration, which follows almost immediately after Caesarea Philippi, three of the disciples glimpse the truth about Jesus in a kind of corporate vision. In Chapter I I suggested that visions were very similar to prophetic dramas, in that they, too, were expressions of the divine will. What Mark describes in this incident is a revelation of the end of the Gospel story – Jesus is seen in glory, and is recognized as superior to both Moses and Elijah, the two great prophets of the past.[6]

We have seen already how Mark uses the prophetic dramas performed by Jesus when he went to Jerusalem. Let us now take note of two actions performed there by other people which Mark clearly interpreted as prophetic dramas. First, we have the story of the woman at Bethany, who anointed Jesus' head.[7] We are told that Jesus himself interpreted what she did as a prophetic drama, with the comment: 'She has anointed my body for burial'. Her action pointed forward to Jesus' death, but it did not make that death inevitable – rather, it was a dramatic sign of what was going to happen. But the interesting thing here is that *Mark* seems to have given another meaning to her action, and interpreted it as a prophetic drama of Jesus' kingship. In both Mark and Matthew it is Jesus' *head* which is anointed, whereas in Luke and John it is his feet.[8] Since in Mark Jesus is proclaimed as King and Messiah through his death, these two themes are clearly linked, and we are probably right in believing that the evangelist interpreted the woman's action as symbolizing not simply Jesus' burial, but also his messianic anointing.

The second action is performed by the high priest when he tears his clothes in response to Jesus' declaration that the Son of man will sit at God's right hand in glory.[9] Like the comment of Caiaphas at John 11.50, which the Fourth Evangelist interprets as an unwitting prophecy of the significance of Jesus' death, Mark may well have seen the high priest's action as an unconscious prophetic drama. The high priest *thinks* he is tearing his clothes because of Jesus' blasphemy: in fact, his action looks forward to the rending of the temple curtain in 15.38; and that, in turn, was an omen of the temple's coming destruction.[10] The high priest's action represents what will happen to the temple. Other actions by Jesus' enemies also have a significance they do not understand. The soldiers mock Jesus, clothing him in purple and hailing him as king:[11] they do not realize that they are proclaiming the truth; the inscription on the cross, written in irony, announces that he is King of the Jews.[12] These actions *function* as prophetic dramas, not because those who do them are prophets, but because God is working through them.

There is one other action which Jesus *refuses* to do – just as he refuses his enemies' demand to perform a sign in Mark 8.11; this is the demand to come down from the cross to prove that he is Messiah and King of Israel. Paradoxically, Jesus' refusal is interpreted by the evangelist as a *true* sign of the significance of what is taking place. His enemies taunt him with the words 'He saved others: himself he cannot save'. Mark's readers will surely understand him to be saying that if Jesus *were* to save himself, he could not save others: Jesus' 'inaction' has become for Mark a prophetic drama of salvation.[13]

2. Matthew

Overall, Matthew's picture is very similar to Mark's. There are only two clear prophetic dramas to add. The first comes in the first chapter, when Joseph gives the name 'Jesus' to Mary's child. Joseph was not himself a prophet, but was carrying out an angel's instructions: as with the children of Isaiah and Hosea, it is the *meaning* of the name – 'Yahweh saves' – that is significant, for 'he will save his people from their sins'.[14]

The other true prophetic drama comes in Matt. 21.14. Immediately after telling us how Jesus drove the merchants out of the temple, Matthew relates how the blind and the lame came to him in the temple and he cured them. The exclusion of one group from the temple and the entry of another forms an interesting contrast when we remember the story in II Samuel 5 of how King David, when attacking Jerusalem, was taunted by its inhabitants, who said that even the blind and the lame could keep him out. David attacked the city and took it; therefore there is a saying, we are told, 'The blind and the lame shall not come into the house' (II Sam. 5.8). But now the blind and the lame come to Jesus in the temple, and far from driving them out, as he has just driven out the merchants, Jesus welcomes them by healing them. What then does the prophetic drama mean? Does Matthew think of it as indicating that from now on no one will be excluded from the worshipping community because of physical infirmity?[15] The fact that Jesus is hailed as Son of David in the next verse suggests that he is seen here as one who is greater than David and who reverses David's ban.

There are two other incidents unique to Matthew which are worthy of note. It is possible to argue that the infancy narrative of the visit of the magi in 2.1–12 *functions* as a prophetic drama, since it signifies the homage which will be paid to Christ by the Gentiles; similarly, the resurrection of the saints in 27.52f. points forward to Jesus' resurrection and the future resurrection of believers: but neither of these events was in any sense *performed* as a prophetic drama.

As in Mark, the miracles are understood as indications as to who Jesus is. His exorcisms and healings are seen – somewhat surprisingly – as the fulfilment of Isa. 53.4.[16] When John the Baptist sends messengers enquiring if he is the one to come, Jesus replies in language reminiscent of various passages in

Isaiah.[17] Similar language is used in the summary of healings in
15.30f. The miracles are thus clear signs that Jesus is the
fulfilment of prophetic hopes. Like Mark, Matthew stresses the
slowness of the disciples to discern these signs of who Jesus is,
but he does so in his own way, by omitting the story of the blind
man who is healed in two stages, so leaving the stories of
the Pharisees' demand for a sign, the disciples' failure to comprehend Jesus' words about leaven, and the incident at Caesarea
Philippi, where Peter grasps the truth, in sequence.[18]

Finally, we should note Matthew's obvious interest in showing Jesus as someone greater than Moses: the slaughter of the
innocents and the return from Egypt are obvious examples of
Moses typology.[19] The Sermon on the Mount – delivered by
Jesus *from* the mountain – reflects Matthew's belief that Jesus'
teaching is superior to that of Moses. That idea is stressed
particularly in the series of antitheses, in 5.21–48. But however
superior Jesus may be, the model of a prophet is still relevant to
Matthew's understanding of him.

3. Luke

In Luke, we find two clear prophetic dramas in his nativity
story: the naming of John and the naming of Jesus. Both names
are given on the instructions of the angel, and Luke describes
both naming ceremonies as significant.[20] He does not explain the
meaning of either name, but the Benedictus spells out the
significance of the name John, 'Yahweh has shown favour',[21]
and the Magnificat expounds the meaning of Jesus, 'Yahweh
saves'.[22]

Jesus himself is portrayed as acting like a prophet throughout
much of the Gospel. Luke places the account of Jesus' visit to
the synagogue in Nazareth at the very beginning of his
ministry.[23] Jesus reads from Isaiah 61 and announces its fulfilment in himself: he is the prophet in whom God's Spirit is at
work. In the ensuing discourse, he declares that no prophet is
welcome in his own home town, and mentions the fact that both
Elijah and Elisha were sent to Gentiles. The following chapters

spell out the way in which Isaiah 61 is fulfilled – Jesus proclaims the good news of God's Kingdom, heals the sick, sets men and women free from demons, proclaims good news to the poor and hungry and raises a widow's son from the dead – a story reminiscent of similar feats attributed to Elijah and Elisha.[24] The people's reaction to this last incident is to declare: 'A great prophet has risen among us.' Immediately afterwards, John the Baptist sends messengers enquiring whether or not Jesus is the One who is to come, whereupon Jesus heals people with various illnesses, including many who were blind – the one item in the quotation of Isaiah 61 that is as yet unfulfilled – and instructs the messengers to tell John what they have seen.[25] In Matthew's version of this story, Jesus replies to the messengers straight away, without pausing to perform healing miracles, but both evangelists clearly see the miracles as 'signs' that Jesus is the One whom the prophets expected.

Throughout these early chapters, Luke's emphasis is on what Jesus *did*. To be sure, he includes the Sermon on the Plain, but in his version, so much shorter than Matthew's Sermon on the Mount, the Sermon serves to fulfil Jesus' claim that he has come to proclaim the good news to the poor. There is no doubt that Luke saw Jesus as fulfilling the role of a prophet – in particular, the role of Elijah. In 9.51 we are told that the time was drawing near for Jesus to be taken up, a phrase reminiscent of what happened to Elijah, and immediately following we are told how two disciples wanted to call down fire from heaven to destroy the inhospitable Samaritans. This story is reminiscent of one told about Elijah in II Kings 1.9–12 – though that describes how Elijah *did* call down fire from heaven. It is followed, a few verses later, by the account of Jesus' call of two men who want to tidy things up at home before they follow him.[26] This story contains several echoes of the account of Elijah's call of Elisha in I Kings 19.19–21.[27]

In Luke, Jesus seems largely to have taken over the role of Elijah from John the Baptist. True, the angel tells Zechariah in 1.17 that John is to go before the Lord in the spirit and power of Elijah. True, in 7.27, Jesus is said to have identified John with the messenger described in Mal.3.1. Yet Luke fails to use two statements attributed to Jesus by Mark and Matthew which identify John with Elijah: he omits the conversation between Jesus and his disciples following the Transfiguration where Elijah is said to have come already;[28] and he does not include the saying attributed to Jesus in Matt. 11.14 where John is clearly identified with Elijah. Although John the Baptist to some extent fulfils the role of Elijah in Luke, part of that role is reserved for Jesus himself, and when we remember the parallelism drawn between John and Jesus in Luke 1–2, this is not, after all, so surprising.

But from 10.1 onwards, reminiscences of Elijah fade from the picture. If any of the prophets is in Luke's mind as he tells of Jesus' journey to Jerusalem it must surely be Moses. Some forty years ago, C.F. Evans[29] suggested that Luke 9.51–18.14 was modelled on the book of Deuteronomy, and the wanderings of Israel through the wilderness. Some of his parallels are more convincing than others, but if Evans is at all correct in his interpretation, the interesting question arises, *why* should Luke have constructed his travel narrative in this way? Could it be because he wished to present Jesus, not simply as a new and greater Elijah, but as a new and greater Moses? But the emphasis must be on the word *greater*, since at the end of the day, neither role is great enough to describe Jesus. In Luke 9, Elijah is mentioned specifically twice, in the summaries of popular opinion about who Jesus is (vv.8,19), all of which are dismissed as inadequate at Caesarea Philippi. At the Transfiguration, both Moses and Elijah appear and converse with Jesus about his coming 'exodus' (v.31), an extraordinary word to use for Jesus' death, but one that shows clearly that Luke is thinking of his death and resurrection as a Second Exodus, and thus of Jesus himself as in some sense a successor to Moses. But the voice from the cloud identifies Jesus as God's Son, and therefore superior to both Moses and Elijah.

In the final chapter of Luke, the double theme of Jesus as both the fulfilment of prophecy and himself a prophet reappears. The men in dazzling garments who met the women at the tomb reminded them of Jesus' own prophecies of his death and resurrection (24.6f.). The two disciples walking to Emmaus said of Jesus that he had been 'a prophet mighty in deed and word' (v.19), whereupon Jesus, 'beginning from Moses and from all the prophets, interpreted to them in all the scriptures the things concerning himself' (v.27). Later in the same chapter he reminds the eleven disciples of the words he had spoken to them – namely how everything written in the Law of Moses and the prophets and the psalms about himself must be fulfilled (v.44): here he is seen to be both a prophet and the one about whom the prophets and others wrote, since the events in Jerusalem have fulfilled his own words as well as those of scripture. Jesus is thus proved to be the prophet like Moses promised in Deut. 18.21f.[30]

4. John

We turn, finally, to the Fourth Gospel. Here, too, the theme of Jesus as a second Moses is clearly an important one. We have already noted the references to 'the prophet':[31] in 1.21 John the Baptist denies that *he* is the prophet who is to come, while in 6.14 and 7.40 the crowd concludes that Jesus is. And though 'Prophet' is an inadequate title for Jesus, it expresses part of the truth about him, since he is the one who, like the prophet foretold by Moses, speaks the words that God gives him.[32] He is, then, in the confession attributed to Philip, the one of whom Moses wrote in the Law.[33] Throughout the Gospel there are many contrasts and parallels with Moses, spelling out a theme found already in the Prologue, where it is based on Exodus 33–34:[34] the law was given through Moses, but grace and truth have come through Jesus Christ; Moses was unable to see God, but Christ, who is close to God, has revealed him in his fullness. In the rest of the Gospel the parallels with Moses are sometimes explicit, as in the references to the serpent in 3.14 and to the manna in 6.30–33, 48–51; elsewhere, in the reference to Jesus as the source of water in 7.37–39 and in the Farewell Discourse in chapters 13–17, it is implicit.[35] In a sense, the whole Gospel demonstrates how the Law given by Moses has been fulfilled in Christ, since he embodies all that the Law was, and worship is now centred on him. Yet this *is* a fulfilment, not an overthrow, since the scriptures testify to Christ; if the Jews believed Moses they would believe Jesus, since Moses wrote about him, but since they do not believe Moses they do not believe Jesus' words (another reference to Deut. 18.18).[36]

It is well known that the term *sēmeia* is an important one for the Fourth Evangelist, and that he uses it in a way markedly different from that in which it is handled by the other three evangelists. Nevertheless, the word *can* be used with a negative sense in John, in exactly the same way as in the other Gospels. We have noted John 2.18 and 6.30 already[37] – two occasions when Jesus is asked to perform a sign: the first demand follows immediately after his prophetic action in the temple, the second after the feeding of the crowd and the crossing of the water, but in each case his opponents fail to understand the significance of his actions. John is here playing on the different meanings of the word *sēmeion*. On each occasion, Jesus' opponents demand a *sēmeion, an authenticating miracle*, because they have failed to see the true significance of the *sēmeion* – that is, the prophetic action – that Jesus has already done. In driving the merchants out of the temple and overthrowing the money-changers' tables, Jesus was performing a prophetic drama, whose significance, John tells us, related not simply to the destruction of the temple, but to Jesus' own death and resurrection. When *these* events take place, men and women will know that his prophetic action was a true prophecy. On the second occasion, the feeding of the crowd leads the people to try to make Jesus king, and his miraculous crossing of the lake leads to utter amazement. Nevertheless, in 6.26 we find Jesus commenting: 'You seek me, *not* because you saw the signs, but because you ate the bread and were satisfied.' In other words, the crowd were interpreting his actions at an earthly level, as so often in John, and failing to see their true significance: they did not realize that they *were* signs. Hence their absurd request in vv.30f.: 'What sign do you do, *so that we may believe in you?* What work are you doing?

Our fathers ate bread in the wilderness, even as scripture says.'
They, too, have eaten bread, but they have failed to recognize
the sign.

There are two further negative remarks concerning signs in
John. The first, in 4.48, has Jesus exclaiming: 'Will none of you
believe, unless you see signs and wonders?' This is similar to the
demands in 2.18 and 6.30. In the second, at 12.37, the author
comments on the failure of the Jews to believe in Jesus, in spite
of the many signs that he had done: once again, the signs were
there, but the people had failed to see their true significance.

On far more occasions, however, John – *unlike* the Synoptic
evangelists – uses the word *sēmeion* in a *positive* sense. But we
should not be misled by this into thinking that he therefore has
a different interpretation of Jesus' actions, for the difference
between John and the Synoptics is a difference of terminology
rather than of meaning: as so often, John makes explicit what is
implicit in the other Gospels.

It is clear that for John, the purpose of the *sēmeia* is that they
lead men and women to believe in Jesus. Every use of the term
sēmeion for one of Jesus' prophetic actions leads to a statement
about belief – either to the effect that men and women believed
in him or that they failed to believe in him.[38]

There are two occasions when John specifically describes an
action of Jesus as a sign: both of these follow miracles. The first
comment comes after the changing of water into wine: in 2.11
he writes: 'This beginning of signs Jesus made in Cana of
Galilee, and manifested his glory, and his disciples believed in
him.' Like some of the prophetic actions in the Old Testament,
the changing of the water into wine is clearly a manifestation of
divine power – though, typically, John sees it as a manifestation
of *Jesus'* glory – i.e. a manifestation of *who Jesus is*. This
particular sign is a key to the significance of Jesus' person.
Unlike the other Johannine signs we have just considered, this
miracle is apparently recognized as a sign by those who knew
about it, since we are told that it led the disciples to believe in
Jesus.

The second comment comes in 4.54, following the healing of

the official's son, a miracle which had led the man and his whole household to believe; and this, we are told, 'was the second sign which Jesus did after coming out of Judaea into Galilee'.

Strangely, the evangelist has not numbered the other signs in his Gospel – though commentators have not been slow to count them for him![39] What he *does* do is to remark from time to time on the fact that the signs Jesus performed led men and women to believe in him. The first of these comments follows almost immediately after Jesus' 'cleansing' of the temple, though it clearly refers to more than this incident: 'many believed in his name, because they saw the signs that he was doing' (2.23). Probably John is thinking of the healing miracles, even though he has not yet described any of them. Immediately following this, he tells us how Nicodemus came to Jesus by night, declaring 'Rabbi, we know that you are a teacher sent by God, for no one could do signs such as you do unless God were with him' (3.2). In John 6, we are told that 'a large crowd followed him, because they saw the signs that he was doing on the sick' (v.2); after relating the story of how Jesus fed them all, John comments: 'When the people saw the sign that he had done, they began to say, "Surely this must be the prophet who is to come into the world" (v.14). A slightly different conclusion is drawn in 7.31, where we are told that many in the crowd believed in Jesus, saying, 'When the Messiah comes, will he do more signs than this man has done?' The puzzling thing about this comment is, of course, that we have no evidence that the Messiah was expected to do 'signs': signs were the province of the prophets. Three things may explain the comment here: first, there may well have been a blurring between the various eschatological figures, and an amalgamation of their characteristics;[40] second, it would not be surprising if it seemed necessary for the Messiah to perform 'authenticating miracles'; and third, by the time John was writing, the crucial question being debated between Jew and Christian was whether or not Jesus was the Messiah. Needless to say, all John's comments regarding Jesus' signs and the reaction of men and women to them reflect the debates taking place in his own time: Christians saw Jesus' actions as 'signs' of God's activity through him, while non-believers saw him as a deceiver of the people. For the Christian community, the miracles were now functioning as 'authenticating miracles'.

This debate is clearly reflected in chapter 9, in the argument between the Pharisees and the blind man. In v.16, the Pharisees declare, 'This man is not from God, since he does not observe the sabbath', but others reply, 'How can a man who is a sinner do such signs?' In 11.47ff., the chief priests and Pharisees hold a consultation about what they can do, since 'This man is performing many signs. If we allow him to go on like this, everyone will believe in him.' Signs, when properly understood, lead to belief. In 12.18, we are told that the crowd flocked to meet Jesus as he entered Jerusalem, 'because they heard that he had performed this sign' – the sign, that is, of raising Lazarus from the dead. And finally, at the end of the Gospel, the evangelist sums up his purpose in writing in these words: 'There were indeed many other signs that Jesus did in the presence of his disciples, which are not recorded in this book. But these are recorded *in order that you may believe that Jesus is the Messiah, the Son of God.*'[41]

Signs, properly understood, lead to belief in Jesus. But does anyone truly comprehend the meaning of the signs until after the resurrection? The answer is, of course, 'no' – and that is because no one comes to full belief in him until after the resurrection. The passages we have just looked at, in which John remarks that people saw Jesus' signs and believed in him, illustrate the double nuance of the word *sēmeia*. In terms of public reaction to Jesus, his signs are functioning simply at the level of authenticating miracles: the people see mighty works and are impressed. Let us glance at those passages again. In 2.23, 'many believed in his name, because they saw the signs that he was doing'. In 3.2, Nicodemus declares 'no one could do signs such as you do unless God were with him'. In 6.2, the crowd 'saw the signs that he was doing on the sick', and in v.14, 'when the people saw the sign that he had done, they began to say "Surely this must be the prophet who is to come into the world" '. In 7.31, the crowd ask whether the Messiah can be expected to 'do more signs than this man has done'. In 9.16, people ask 'How can a man who is a sinner do such signs?' In 11.47f., Jesus' opponents are afraid that if they allow him to go on doing signs, 'everyone will believe in him'. In 12.18, the crowd greet Jesus 'because they heard that he had performed a sign'. Only with 20.30f. are we told their full significance. The signs do indeed 'authenticate' Jesus. But it is not simply as a prophet, nor even merely as the Messiah, but as Messiah *and Son of God*. And because Jesus is Son of God, the signs are at one and the same time epiphanies of who God is and who Jesus is. It is only when the signs are seen as *manifestations of Jesus' glory* that they are properly understood.[42]

Not surprisingly, however, the word *sēmeia* is not usually attributed to Jesus himself. In the Fourth Gospel, Jesus speaks repeatedly of his 'works'. Whenever he does so, his works are clearly identified with *the works of God*:[43] we are invited to see God at work in Jesus' actions – that is the true significance of the 'signs'.

The different levels at which a miracle can be comprehended are well illustrated by the story of the healing of the blind man in John 9. At one level, the healing can be treated as an 'authenticating miracle', demonstrating that Jesus comes from God and cannot be dismissed as a sinner.[44] Yet this is certainly not its purpose! It represents a misunderstanding of the sign's true significance. At the deeper level of Johannine interpretation, the miracle serves as a revelation of who Jesus is, so that the blind man is taken from one step of faith to another until he finally confesses faith in Jesus and worships him as Lord.[45] With this acknowledgment of Jesus, the true purpose of the miracle is understood to be the revelation that Jesus' activity is nothing less than the work of God himself.[46]

It is time to look a little more closely at those actions of Jesus which John wants us to see as 'signs' – that is, as prophetic actions which point us to the significance of what is taking place in the ministry of Jesus.

5. The Johannine signs

The first sign, so John tells us, was the miracle of changing water into wine which took place in Cana of Galilee (2.1–11). John gives us hints of its significance in his concluding comment that through it Jesus 'manifested his glory', as well as in the remark attributed to Jesus himself that his hour had not yet come. In John, Jesus' 'hour' is the hour of his death, which is seen as a glorification.[47] This particular prophetic drama, then, has something to do with the revelation of Jesus' glory which takes place through his death and resurrection. There is a further hint as to the sign's meaning in the reference to the fact that the water stored in the six stone jars was intended for the Jewish rites of purification: the gospel is the eschatological *fulfilment* of Judaism, not its opponent, but Jewish lustrations are nevertheless being *contrasted* with the heady wine of the Gospel.

Immediately following, we have another prophetic drama, this time in the temple at Jerusalem. John does not describe this as a sign – perhaps because its significance was not seen at the time, and so it did not lead anyone to believe: on the contrary, the Jews promptly demanded a sign of Jesus' authority, and it was only much later, we are told, that the disciples remembered and believed Jesus' words of explanation. For the reader of the Gospel, however, the incident does function as a sign. Like the Synoptic evangelists, John sees this incident as a prophecy of the destruction of the temple, and he makes this explicit in the words 'Destroy this temple, and in three days I will raise it up' (v.19) – a saying which in Matthew and Mark is attributed to Jesus by his opponents at the so-called trial before the Sanhedrin.[48] But John immediately seems to reject this interpretation, since in v.21 he says that Jesus 'was speaking about the temple of his body'. It is perhaps not so much a rejection of the literal interpretation as a weaving together of the various interpretations already hinted at in Mark and Matthew: the Jews will indeed destroy the 'temple' of Jesus' earthly body, but he will rise again; the temple in Jerusalem will also be destroyed, but the worship which took place there will be replaced by something else.

What that is to be is spelt out in the next two chapters, where Jesus converses first with Nicodemus, one of the Pharisees, about the need to be born from above, through water and the Spirit, if one is to enter God's Kingdom, and then with a Samaritan woman, about the true worship of God which is going to replace worship both at Jerusalem and at the Samaritan sanctuary at Gerizim. Both these chapters pick up the central theme of the two prophetic actions in John 2 – namely, that the practices and worship of Judaism are going to be replaced by Christian worship, a replacement that comes about through the death and resurrection of Jesus. In both conversations, the importance of believing in Jesus is underlined,[49] and in the first, this theme of believing in Jesus is focussed on the salvation that comes through his death and resurrection.[50]

Here are two signs, then, the significance of which is spelt out in two conversations. But John uses various levels of symbolism, and his Gospel is full of double meanings and metaphors. Some of these are purely verbal – e.g. in John 3 Jesus speaks of *pneuma*, and his teaching plays on the double significance of that word – 'wind' and 'spirit'. But in v.14 we have a reference to a *past* action which is now given a new interpretation, and is seen as pointing forward to the crucifixion: 'Just as Moses lifted up the serpent in the wilderness, so must the Son of man be lifted up.' Moses' action in raising the serpent is now interpreted as a prophetic drama – not simply a prophecy of Jesus' death, but a prophecy of the salvation that will come through it, since those who were bitten by serpents and looked at the bronze serpent were reputedly healed.[51] In John 4 we have a subsidiary prophetic action, symbolizing once again the way in which the old is giving way to the new, the temporary to the permanent. Again, it is not performed by Jesus himself, but by the Samaritan woman – if, indeed, she does respond to Jesus' request in v.7 to give him a drink. The water she draws from the well symbolizes the living water that Jesus offers to those who believe in him.

The pattern of signs, followed by explanatory discourses, found in John 2–12, is well known, and has been discussed many times. At the end of John 4 and the beginning of John 5 we have two healing miracles, in which Jesus gives life to two people who were as good as dead: the first, in 4.46–54, which leads men and women to believe, is specifically described as a sign. Not surprisingly, the discourse in 5.19–47 is about Jesus as the giver of life. In John 6, the feeding of the crowd and the walking on the lake are followed by a discourse in which Jesus is revealed as the living bread that came down from heaven. All these signs point forward to the life which will be given to men and women through the death of Jesus.

In John 7, Jesus goes to Jerusalem for the Feast of Tabernacles: John mentions no signs – though in 7.31, the crowd comment on how many signs Jesus has done. In vv. 37–39, however, we are told that on the last day of the festival, Jesus claims to be the source of living water for those who believe in him.[52] Commentators find the background for this in the ceremonies that took place at the festival, since each morning a pitcher was filled with water at the fountain of Gihon, while Isa. 12.3 was recited; the water was then taken in procession to the temple and poured out on the altar of burnt-offering. The ritual was apparently linked with the water that gushed from the rock in the wilderness[53] and with the prophecy of water flowing from Jerusalem in Zech.14.8. Jesus' enigmatic saying in 7.37–39 appears to be based on that ritual – in other words, it interprets the action of pouring out the water as *though* that were a prophetic drama. The action itself, however, is not mentioned, and we thus have no sign. Nevertheless, Jesus' words lead some in the crowd to declare 'This is the prophet', and others 'This is the Messiah'. But if we are right in suggesting that the saying in 7.37–39 was at some stage the interpretation of an action which was seen as prophetic, why is there no reference to that action? Was it because the evangelist assumed that his readers would *know* what happened on the last day of the feast? Or was it because he wanted to link Jesus' words to the flow of water from his side which takes place in 19.34? For there, in the piercing of the body of Jesus by a soldier, causing blood and water to gush out, we have an action which most commentators link with Jesus' saying in John 7.[54] And the evangelist clearly regards this as an important sign, since he tells us in 19.35 that an eye-witness has testified to its truth, in order that the readers of the Gospel may believe. Perhaps he expects us to remember the saying of 7.37–39 when we come to the sign itself in John 19.

Interestingly, the sayings about Jesus' blood in 6.53–56 are also interpretative comments without a prophetic action; they fit uneasily into the exposition of the bread in the rest of the chapter, which is based on the miracle of the feeding. We can see why the sayings are recorded here, in John's equivalent to the Synoptic eucharistic discourse, but there is no prophetic action with a cup of wine for them to interpret. But these words, too, find their appropriate 'prophetic action' in the incident in 19.34, when blood and water flow from Jesus' side.

John 8 picks up the other great theme associated with Tabernacles, that of light: Jesus declares that he is the light of the world (v.12). This theme is then enacted in the prophetic drama of the opening of a blind man's eyes in John 9. The debate between the blind man, his neighbours and parents, the Pharisees and Jesus himself, draws out the meaning of this sign as the man's faith develops, until finally he worships Jesus and declares 'Lord, I believe' (9.38). Jesus' final words confirm that though the blind man has gained his sight, the Pharisees are blind. The theme of this chapter is parallel to the stories that Mark puts side by side in 8.22–30, but as usual, John makes explicit what in the Synoptics is implicit.

In John 10, Jesus describes himself as the good shepherd who cares for his sheep. Again, we seem to have metaphorical language without a prophetic action. But in v.11 Jesus points forward to what *will be* a prophetic action, in the words 'I am the good shepherd: the good shepherd lays down his life for his sheep', and once again, that saying interprets the significance of Jesus' death.

In John 11 comes the story of the raising of Lazarus at

Bethany – a sign whose meaning is spelt out in the declaration that Jesus is the resurrection and the life (v.25). Also set in Bethany is the story of the anointing of Jesus.[55] In the Fourth Gospel this act is performed by Mary, Lazarus' sister, and Jesus' comment interprets it as a dramatic action prophesying his burial. Unlike the stories in Mark and Matthew, where the unnamed woman anoints Jesus' head, Mary here pours the ointment over Jesus' feet, a decidedly strange thing to do, not simply because she was the hostess, but because it was not customary to anoint a person's feet. In Luke, too, it is Jesus' feet that are anointed, but there it is not so strange, since the woman is a sinner, and perhaps dares do no more than touch his feet; in Luke's version of the story the woman's action is seen as an indication of her repentance and her love for Jesus, and is not linked with his death.[56] Did John miss the possible allusion to a royal anointing, or did he deliberately reject it? Did he simply have a different tradition from Mark and Matthew? Or does the anointing of the feet point forward in other significant ways to the death of Jesus? First, because anointing the feet of a living person was not normal, and therefore more readily suggests the symbolism of anointing a corpse.[57] Secondly, because the anomalous scene reminds us of the dramatic action performed by Jesus himself in the following chapter, when he washes the feet of his disciples.

The anointing is followed immediately by another prophetic drama staged by Jesus – the entry into Jerusalem. John spells out its significance: Jesus is hailed as King of Israel (12.13) and his action in riding on a donkey is said to be the fulfilment of Zech. 9.9; John remarks that the disciples failed to comprehend this at the time, but understood its significance after Jesus had been glorified, so reminding us that the drama points to a reality that will be fully realized only later. The arrival of Greeks who wish to see Jesus in v.20 can also be seen as a prophetic drama. Apparently they are left standing outside, while a message is taken to Jesus by Philip and Andrew. Jesus then declares, 'The hour has come for the Son of man to be glorified; truly I tell you, unless a grain of wheat falls into the earth and dies, it remains a single grain, but if it dies, it bears much fruit' (vv.23f.). John does not tell us why Jesus speaks in this way, nor whether the Greeks ever succeed in seeing him. Presumably they cannot see him until he is glorified through death and resurrection: Jesus is the grain of wheat who falls into the earth and dies, in order to bear much fruit. When that happens, the Greeks will be brought in. Till then, they are left on the edge, waiting, since, to use another Johannine metaphor, they are sheep who do not belong to this fold.[58]

However, for Jesus the hour of his glorification has now come (v.23). This theme is elaborated in the rest of John 12. It is the hour which glorifies not only Jesus but also God himself (v.28). Jesus must now be lifted up from the earth (v.32), as he foretold in 3.14. This lifting up on the cross is the supreme sign, and its meaning is indicated by the double meaning of *hupsoō*, 'to lift up'. Jesus' enemies will see the body of a blasphemer, hung from a gibbet, but believers will see his exaltation and the revelation of God's glory. There is a sense in which all the other signs in the Gospel have pointed forward to this great sign. The water turned to wine was specifically linked to the hour of Jesus' glorification, the incident in the temple to his death and resurrection; the healings in John 4 and 5 and the raising of Lazarus in John 11 all reveal the power of Jesus to give life, and all point forward to the resurrection of those who believe in him.[59] The sign of the bread in John 6 looks forward to Jesus' death, as do the sayings about blood and water in John 6 and 7. The man blind from birth who is given his sight by Jesus in John 9 gradually finds faith, until in vv.35–38 he confesses his belief in the Son of man – and in John, the Son of man is, above all else, the one who is lifted up on the cross[60] and glorified.[61] The sayings about the good shepherd who lays down his life for the sheep (10.15) and the grain of wheat that falls into the earth (12.24), like the saying about the serpent lifted up in the wilderness, reach their fulfilment in the crucifixion. The anointing at Bethany is said to relate to his burial (12.7), and after Jesus' entry into Jerusalem as king the evangelist comments that the significance of this event was understood by the disciples only after his glorification. With this hint that we need to look forward to comprehend its meaning we turn to John's account of Jesus' 'trial' by Pilate, which hinges on the question whether or not Jesus is King of the Jews.[62] He is mocked by the soldiers as King and crucified under the inscription 'Jesus of Nazareth, the King of the Jews'.[63] All the Johannine signs, then, focus on the exaltation of Christ on the cross, and all are prophetic dramas, since they portray the significance of Jesus' exaltation on the cross. Each of the signs reveals something of who Jesus is and of what he achieves through his death; each is a 'work' of the one who does the works of his Father. Who Jesus is and what the great work of God is are both finally revealed in the cross, where Jesus and his Father are glorified, and Jesus' saving work is completed.

Another prophetic drama takes place during supper on the last night of Jesus' life.[64] It replaces the breaking of bread and the sharing of wine in the Synoptic Gospels, but its meaning is remarkably similar. Jesus takes off his outer garment, ties a towel round his waist, pours out water into a bowl and begins to wash his disciples' feet. The significance of the drama is plain: the menial task of washing the disciples' feet is a sign of the service Jesus has given them throughout his ministry; the setting, however, links the action specifically with his coming death (13.1–3). We are not surprised, therefore, to find another layer of significance hinted at in the conversation between Jesus and Peter: those who are washed by Jesus have a share with him (v.8), and are wholly cleansed (v.10); what Jesus is doing for his disciples has atoning power. The prophetic action thus reminds us of Jesus' saying in Matt. 20.28//Mark 10.45. But the drama signifies also the mutual service which ought to be shown within the Christian community, and the teaching in vv.12–20 which spells this out is remarkably similar to some of the sayings in the Synoptic tradition.[65] At this level, the incident functions as an acted parable.

Yet another prophetic action follows quickly: in place of the saying in Matthew and Mark that Jesus' betrayer is dipping with him into the same dish,[66] we have a mini-drama in which

Jesus identifies the betrayer by handing him a piece of bread that has been dipped into the communal dish.[67] At one level, this is simply a way of passing information privately to the beloved disciple. But the evangelist then tells us that Satan immediately entered Judas' heart, and that Jesus told him to do what he had to do. It seems that John, who saw Jesus as being in command of events even during the passion, paradoxically interpreted Jesus' action as a kind of commissioning.

As in the Synoptics, the mocking of Jesus (19.1–5) and the *titulus* (19.19–22) are treated as though they were prophetic actions: through his death, Jesus is proclaimed as King. John emphasizes the significance of the *titulus*, telling us that it was written in three languages and that Pilate refused to alter it, declaring 'What I have written I have written'. One prophetic action is something that does not happen: in 19.32f. the soldiers refrain from breaking Jesus' legs – a sign, we are surely meant to understand, that he is the true passover lamb, since he was crucified at the time the passover lambs were sacrificed.

The final prophetic drama is said to have taken place after the resurrection, in the miraculous catch of fish.[68] The evangelist surely sees this as symbolic, but its meaning is obscure, as is the significance of the number of fish caught, one hundred and fifty-three. Perhaps the fact that the story is followed by Jesus' commissioning of Peter indicates that, as in Luke's version, the story symbolizes the task now being given to the disciples to bring men and women into the Christian community.

There is one other incident in the Fourth Gospel which suggests Jesus' use of prophetic drama: it is the story of the woman taken in adultery in 8.1–11. The story does not belong at this point in the narrative, and probably is not Johannine, but it is worth looking at in its own right. From our point of view, the interesting feature of this story is that we are told that Jesus twice stooped down and began writing on the ground (vv. 6,8). The action baffles the commentators: some suggest that he was writing out texts from the Torah;[69] others conclude that he was simply doodling in the sand;[70] but the action of writing is important, and it is repeated. Jeremias included it among Jesus'

'parabolic actions',[71] and Schnackenburg comments that it is 'a
symbolic action which people with a feeling for prophetic signs
could have understood'.[72] T.W. Manson suggested that Jesus
was following the practice of Roman law – writing out the
sentence before pronouncing it,[73] but we expect Jesus to act like
a Jewish prophet, not a Roman judge. The best explanation is
the earliest, given by Ambrose, Augustine and Jerome:[74] Jesus
wrote the words of Jer. 17.13, 'Those who forsake you will be
inscribed in the dust'.[75] The meaning of that passage appears to
be that names inscribed in the dust are quickly erased, and that
those who forsake God will soon be forgotten. The woman's
accusers have all 'forsaken God', since they have refused to
acknowledge that Jesus has been sent by God. The words of
Jesus in v.7 confirm the appropriateness of this interpretation,
and the departure of the men in v.9 adds further support. Jesus'
action, then, is a prophetic drama condemning those who were
trying to trap him.

  If we read on in Jer. 17.13, we find that the words I have
quoted are followed by a parallel line in which God is described
as the source of living water: 'for they have rejected the fountain
of living water, the Lord'. The story of the woman taken in
adultery is found in John at the beginning of John 8, and what
it is doing there is a mystery.[76] But it is worth noting that it
follows immediately after the account of how Jesus taught in the
temple at the Feast of Tabernacles and proclaimed himself to be
the source of living water for those who believed in him: perhaps
somebody noticed the connection between the two stories via
Jer. 17.13, and thought the incident of the woman would fit as
appropriately here as anywhere. The scribes and Pharisees have
been inscribed in the dust and are destined for destruction,
because they have rejected the one who is the source of living
water.

6. Conclusion

All our evangelists clearly believe that Jesus is greater than a
prophet: nevertheless, all four Gospels contain evidence that he

was regarded as a prophet during his lifetime. The fact that Jesus was so regarded is, of course, hardly surprising. What is interesting is that the evidence for this view has been retained, even though it does not coincide with that of the evangelists. The fact that both Matthew and Luke use prophet-typology of Jesus, for example, even though belief in him as a prophet was in their view inadequate, shows how firmly rooted in the tradition this belief was. Both Matthew and Luke use this tradition creatively to show that Jesus was 'a prophet, and *more than* a prophet'.[77] Jesus was seen as a prophet and interpreted as a prophet because he did the things associated with prophets: he was, in Luke's words, seen as 'a prophet mighty *in deed* and word'.

The mighty deeds of Jesus were, above all, his miracles. All four of our evangelists record that Jesus performed miracles, but that he refused to perform *authenticating* miracles. The miracles he *did* perform were primarily acts of salvation, manifestations of divine power, though they serve also as 'prophetic dramas', to signify the even greater salvation which is about to burst in. Yet for those who had the eyes to see, these miracles were also sufficient proof that Jesus was a 'true' prophet acting with authority from God, and thus *served* as 'authenticating miracles' – not, indeed, to outsiders, but to those who already believed in him; just as the 'authenticating' miracles given to Moses persuaded the Hebrews, but not Pharaoh, that Moses was sent by God, so the miracles performed by Jesus were understood by his disciples, but not by those whose hearts were hardened, to be evidence that the Spirit of God was at work in him. For our evangelists, however, the emphasis has shifted, since the gospel they are setting out is the gospel *about* Jesus, and not simply the gospel he proclaimed; the miracles of Jesus are interpreted by them as evidence, not that Jesus is a prophet, but that he is Messiah and Son of God.[78]

Our four evangelists are also agreed in recording that Jesus behaved like a prophet in performing dramatic actions – once again, an indication that we are dealing here with firm historical tradition. These actions were seen as prophetic dramas which represented what God was doing through his ministry. But these, too, were subject to reinterpretation by the evangelists. For them, many of these actions were no longer seen merely as 'prophetic dramas', pointing to events that were taking place in Jesus' ministry or that were about to take place: they, too, came to be seen more and more as manifestations of the significance of Jesus' own person.

The tendency to interpret both miracles and prophetic actions as pointing us to the truth about the identity of Jesus himself, rather than seeing both as part of the message he proclaimed – the gospel about, rather than the gospel of – is seen already in the Synoptic Gospels, but increases in the Fourth Gospel. Jesus' actions are interpreted as 'signs' whose meaning is clear to believers, but is hidden from those without faith. For John, all theses signs point forward to the Cross, where the true identity of the person who does them is finally revealed.

We see, then, that the tension in the Gospels between the proclamation of Jesus and that of the evangelists, which is often summarized in the statement that Jesus proclaimed the Kingdom of God and the early Church proclaimed Jesus, is reflected exactly in the tension between what Jesus himself did and the significance the church saw in his actions. Just as Jesus' parables of the Kingdom were reinterpreted as pointing primarily to his own role, so his prophetic actions (through which the Kingdom was breaking in) were now understood by the evangelists as revealing who and what Jesus is. Prophetic oracle and prophetic action had similar functions in the ministry of Jesus, and both were reinterpreted by the believing community in the same way. This is hardly surprising since, as we saw in Chapter I, prophetic word and prophetic action belong together.[79] In the ministry of Jesus, his words and his actions belong together, and both provoke astonishment regarding his authority;[80] the unity of word and action is summed up above all in the word *Logos*, used in John 1.1 as the key to the whole Gospel.

This exploration of the topic of 'prophetic drama' has reminded us of the importance of looking at the record of what Jesus did, as well as what he said. When we consider his actions as well as his words, then we realize that he must have appeared to his contemporaries to stand firmly in the Jewish prophetic tradition.

But this idea of prophetic drama helps us to understand, not simply Jesus himself, but the way in which the evangelists handled the tradition about him. Even though they came to believe that Jesus was more than a prophet, they continued to see his words and actions, spoken with the authority of God, as spoken and done in the tradition of the prophets, who also proclaimed, in word and action, the message of God to his people.

Appendix

The Lord's Supper as Prophetic Drama

David Stacey

If ever you spend an odd moment looking through a box of old photographs, you may find yourself, without realizing it, in the same uncomfortable position as that of a historical critic. Here is a picture of a chubby little boy, hair askew, trousers at half mast, face covered in jam. How distant he seems, and yet how real to you! You know that the little boy grew up to be what? Maybe a prize-winner at school; maybe a constant worry to his parents. Maybe a highly competent professional something; maybe unemployed. You know all the history and you cannot look at the photograph without being aware of it. But the photograph doesn't show any of this history. It was all hidden in the future when years ago someone clicked the shutter.

This illustrates one of the capital problems of the historical critic. We know all about the history of the Christian church; we know all about the development of Christian theology; we know all about Nicaea and Chalcedon. What we find difficult is to realize that Mark and Paul did not know any of these things. They and all the writers of the New Testament wrote out of a comprehensive ignorance of Christian history. For all they knew the Christian story would turn out utterly different from how it did.

1. The Last Supper

The account of the Last Supper is a supreme illustration of this problem. The Lord's Supper is to all of us a large part of our Christian experience; it is part of our existence as a Christian community; and of course it is invested at all points with theological convictions and with arguments and accretions that have kept theological and liturgical scholars happily, or at times unhappily, employed down through the centuries. But when Jesus gathered with his disciples in that upper room, all this was hidden in the future. Not even the most elementary theological reflection made by the earliest evangelist, or made apparent in the earliest Christian community, could possibly have been present in the minds of the disciples when they sat down together. For them that meal was a Last Supper, the last of many that they had partaken of together. For us, as our liturgy reminds us, it was the first supper, to be repeated millions of times under all kinds of conditions down through the centuries and still, as our present revision of the Service Book reminds us, continuing as a vital part of our tradition today.

I think this fact is clear when we study the text; indeed it was partially clear to the evangelists themselves. Mark, for example, tells us that Jesus sent two of his disciples to make preparations for the Passover. But when we come to the meal itself, the idea of a Passover disappears from view and we have a text that owes more to the worshipping practice of Mark's own Christian community than to any simple historical source. It is as if Mark heaves a sigh at this point and says, 'Everybody will know what I mean by this bit'. Of course they will, because they were repeating it every week in their worship. But did it cross Mark's mind that, by telling it that way, he was drawing a veil over what Jesus and the disciples had actually done in the upper room? The disciples would have known nothing about the regular practice of Mark's church, and their understanding of what was happening could not have been determined in any way by it. It may be of immense interest to *us* to know how the primitive communities celebrated the eucharist, but that means that we have to keep two things separate in our minds. We have to distinguish the world of the early communities from the story of the upper room. We have to study the worship indicated by the texts, while at the same time pining to know what took place before the texts were written, particularly in the creative moment, on that first dramatic occasion, before the actual eucharist was launched into history.

In this lecture I shall be searching for that first occasion, and the method I shall employ is not to work back from the texts as we have them now. That would be the normal method, though, as I have indicated, immensely difficult because of the mountain of later interpretation that has been raised upon them. No, my method will be to try to establish, from studying the background, the conditions under which a group of faithful Jews and their leader would actually have met and what must have happened when they did. There is no doubt that something unique took place in the upper room, something that cannot be explained simply in terms of the background, but we shall appreciate that element all the more if we can see it in the context of the kind of meal that the disciples actually shared on that occasion. What was the precise situation as far as we can know it? That is a very difficult question, but the answer to it will surely shed light on the true nature of the Lord's Supper.

Talk about the precise situation proves to have two senses. One concerns the character of the meal as a Jewish event, a character that would have been common to all similar Jewish meals. The other concerns the situation of the meal in the history of the group, of the common life lived by Jesus and his disciples. Both these have to be taken into consideration when we consider what they would have been doing and thinking.

Every group with a continuing identity quickly develops a language and an ongoing agenda of its own. Every meal carries on from the meal before and the continuity makes communal understanding possible. If, *per impossibile*, Jesus and his disciples had sat down to a meal which had no such continuing agenda and Jesus had broken bread which had no established symbolic meaning, then his words, which were an addendum spoken only on this one occasion, 'Take, eat, this is my body,' would have had very little force for the disciples or anybody else. New meanings can occur only when a language, in which those meanings can be expressed, is already familiar. The first question we have to ask, therefore, is, 'What was the general setting of the meal, what did the disciples expect from it, what was the mood, what was the appropriate form of discourse that would have fitted into the occasion as the disciples understood it?' We can answer those questions both positively and negatively, both in terms of what it must have been like and in terms of what it could not possibly have been like. Let us take the negative first.

Negatively it means that we are wrong to suppose that Jesus entered into a discourse with his disciples about topics that had never been raised among them before, such as that his body was spiritual food, his blood a sacrifice for sin, his death an initiatory offering to found a new covenant. Let me be clear that I am not in any way disparaging these interpretations of the eucharist. I am sure they were made very early and that they are profoundly important for Christian believers today. I am merely saying that they were not the ideas that could have belonged to this meal and that, therefore, they were worked out at a later stage, not expounded in what was spoken and done in the upper room. Similarly, when we come to discuss the words Jesus spoke, we shall have to conclude that he said nothing that would have led his disciples to an intense philosophical discussion of the meaning of the verb 'to be', though intense philosophical discussion has certainly followed on. It was not that kind of moment. They were not that kind of people.

This was a moment in which a great corporate experience was coming to an end, when an association was reaching its climax. We can expect Jesus to look backwards, to underline what he had said before, to stress future responsibilities, but not to produce a series of new revelations that at this point in time his hearers would have found bewildering. It was a time for penetrating simplicities, for the elemental realities of their relationship to be made clear.

Now to turn to the positive. What must the situation have been? Positively we shall see Jesus as the charismatic leader of a devoted band bringing their long and intense relationship to a meaningful, if tragic, end. He was doing it in a way that the leader of any Jewish company would, though, of course, he was doing more than that. He was performing a common action, but elevating that action so that it became unique to him and to that moment.

2. Meal symbolism

I want to allude to two things. First, meals, including semi-formal meals, had a large place in Hebrew culture. The way people eat together is an important factor in all anthropological study, for rarely does corporate eating appear as a purely neutral, unstructured, and functional act. Eating together means recognizing a common need and participating together in some material substance that satisfies that need. Eating together always created a bond, and it is legitimate to ask what the precise nature of that bond was. So the meal in the upper room would have been a significant event for Jesus and the disciples quite apart from anything special that he said or did.

In parenthesis let me say that it will be well for us if we pay attention to actions rather than words. Under intense emotion one does not take in much of the spoken word, least of all spoken words that are complex, using ideas that belong to other, extraneous contexts. But one does remember actions. Things that were done stick in the mind because they don't have to be thought about calmly and abstractly. They can be accomplished and experienced and appropriated without thought. So I want to concentrate on what Jesus and his disciples did rather than on what was said.

Secondly, and this is the main point to which this paper is directed, I want to suggest that we may be helped to understand the incident if we think of it in terms of prophetic drama. If we assume, and I think we may assume, that Jesus was seen by his disciples as a figure in the prophetic tradition, however much greater than the prophets he may have been, then we have a key to guide us in the way that his actions would have been understood. He was a prophet using a prophet's dramatic methods. That means that we have all the examples of prophetic drama in the Old Testament to guide us.

Now let us take a closer look at these two points. First, the central feature of Jewish worship in the Old Testament was a meal, the *zebah s^elamim*, traditionally rendered 'peace offering'. This was the most frequent of all the Jewish sacrifices. After the blood was offered to Yahweh and the priests had received their share, the carcase of the animal was returned to the worshippers who consumed it together as part of a religious feast that bound them together and linked them all in a bond of peace to their God. The great domestic festival, the Passover, has always been a meal eaten in similar circumstances and with similar intent. Meals figure largely in the ministry of Jesus, both before and after the resurrection. Fundamentally meals stand for together-ness and reconciliation between the participants, and between the participants and Yahweh. The formalities varied, of course, but if we think of the common, formal meal, taken in the home, there was a more or less regular procedure. At the beginning the paterfamilias would take bread, say a blessing to Yahweh over the bread, break it into fragments, and share it among the participants. At the end of the meal he might similarly take a cup of wine, bless God, and share that.

There is much discussion of whether the Last Supper was a Passover or not and the issue remains unresolved. There is no way in which we can become embroiled in that discussion here, but there is no need. The procedure I have just outlined would have taken place whether the meal was a Passover or not. Certainly there would be additional features if it was a Passover, but they are not all that important to us. If the meal was not a Passover, it remained the Passover season and the Passover mood would still be abroad. What we know as the Christmas spirit is not confined to 25 December. So the crucial ideas of Passover would have been relevant, whatever the precise nature of the meal. We shall come back to this in a moment.

At this point I want to call upon the researches of David Daube, the eminent Jewish scholar, because he has made a most careful study of this phenomenon of breaking bread and come up with what I think we must recognize as a suggestion that comes out of the heart of Judaism.[1] Daube concentrates on an element in the Passover, the breaking and distribution of an unleavened loaf referred to by the mysterious and untranslatable word *afikoman*. There has been much discussion about this term. Everybody knows what was done; the discussion concerns what the word means. Daube says that it is a transliteration of a Greek participle meaning 'he that comes'. In other words the loaf stands in the first place for Israel, for the eschatological Israel, but especially for the solidarity of Israel in the Messianic figure who would surely come.

Few people agree with Daube absolutely, but it is hard to believe that he is completely wrong. And if he is right simply in his contention that there was a messianic element to the sharing of bread at the Passover, then this cannot be irrelevant to the words of Jesus, 'This is my body', whether the meal was a Passover or not. The disciples would already have in their minds the notion that the bread they were sharing stood for Israel, the messianic community. Now Jesus was saying, 'This is me' and, even more stunningly, 'I am giving what I am to you'.

3. Prophetic drama

Now let us, for a moment, leave meal symbolism on one side and think of Jesus' general behaviour in terms of prophetic drama. I do not have time to argue that Jesus was seen by everybody in the category of prophet, but that does seem to me to be a reasonable assumption. Many other titles are heaped upon him by later christological affirmation in the New Testament, but the crowds, who came to hear him teach, would surely have seen him as a new kind of prophetic person, at the very least. The notion of messiahship may have been raised, but that would not necessarily displace the prophetic persona, especially as Jesus seemed to perform prophetic actions such as his entry into Jerusalem and his clearing out of the temple. So the disciples would have been quite ready to read his actions in the upper room as prophetic actions, which means that we have to take a closer look at prophetic actions in general.

Some of you will know that I have spent a lot of time trying to explain this phenomenon in a recent book about prophetic drama.[2] Let me summarize what I mean by prophetic drama. Prophets occasionally turn to dramatic action, as when Isaiah walked naked or Jeremiah smashed his pot. These actions are usually quite simple and mundane. Ezekiel is different in that he is less simple, but he is different in this regard all across the board. Occasionally these actions are not specially contrived, but everyday, oft-repeated actions, that are deliberately taken over and used as prophetic material. For example, all children were given names at birth, but once or twice the naming ceremony was elevated into a very special message. Wrapping a garment around someone was a common adoption ceremony, but when Elisha wrapped his cloak round Elisha, he was investing him for a lifetime's calling. The essence of the action is not its complexity but the deliberation and purposefulness with which, in its simplicity, it was carried out.

The act is carried out under a sense of divine compulsion. Because of our love of analytic methods, we are inclined to stress the distinctions between oracle, action and fulfilment, but this is an error. Yahweh who gives the oracle also requires the action and supplies the fulfilment. All three are part of one divine reality. In most cases the action is a miniature of the larger event to which it points. Smashing the pot represents smashing the city and everybody would be quite clear about that. It is not necessary for all three elements to be present. The action may be accompanied by an oracle, but it does not need to be; it can speak for itself. Always, however, the action points to a larger event, the fall of a city, the end of a nation. The most simple and mundane act can indicate a disaster of international proportions. All elements, the word, the act, the colossal fulfilment, come from the specific intention of Yahweh.

It is easy to assume that the purpose of the action is to aid communication, but the facts are rather more complex. Some actions are harder to interpret than the oracles; some actions don't have any interpretation in words at all. It is better to assume that the word, the action, and the fulfilment are all given by Yahweh. None of the three, where all three are present, is subsidiary to any of the others in the divine purpose.

It was also common for prophets to involve other people, often unwitting, in their dramatic acts. Jeremiah used the Rechabites in Jeremiah 35 and the Rechabites' ignorance of how they were being used was almost essential to the intent. No matter what the strain, they would not compromise their identity. Baruch may have understood something of Jeremiah's intention in writing the scroll; but it is certain that the children of Hosea and Isaiah could have had no idea why they were given such elaborate names. However, knowing or unknowing, all these people were involved in the dramatic action. Just what the disciples understood at the material moment we shall never know, but they were involved in the drama of the upper room and indeed were a significant part of it.

The use of material objects is a regular feature of prophetic drama. Samuel's robe, Ahijah's cloak, Elijah's mantle are all important and they are used in different ways. And there are arrows, slates, waistcloths, yokes, bricks, and so on. The use of bread, therefore, in the upper room is entirely in line with the traditions of prophetic drama. It is common to identify the object with some other reality for the purpose of the drama. Jeremiah's pot stands for Jerusalem; his loincloth stands for the pride and privilege of Judah. In Ezek. 5.5 Ezekiel's shorn hair *is* Jerusalem. So there is nothing unusual about the upper room formula, 'This is my body'. The bread is identified with the person of Jesus for the purpose of the drama.

One of the critical features of prophetic drama was the mimetic element. Jeremiah wore a yoke and Hananiah broke it; Zedekiah made horns; Elijah threw a cloak around Elisha; Isaiah walked naked. In every case it is reasonable to ask the questions, 'What, in the common fund of understanding, would this action indicate?' 'What would the action suggest to the onlookers?' Jeremiah's yoke 'worked' because the yoke was a known symbol of serfdom; horns were a symbol of strength; Isaiah's nakedness was a recognized symbol of humiliation. Similarly the breaking of the bread was a known symbol of fellowship and sharing. This is a most important factor in relation to the upper room, one that has not been pressed as hard as it should have been.

Often the mimetic element was complemented by a verbal explanation. 'Just as my servant Isaiah has walked naked and barefoot for three years . . . so shall the king of Assyria lead away the Egyptians as captives.' Likewise with Jeremiah's pot, 'So will I break this people and this city.' There is a similar formula in the account of the upper room. We don't always have these verbal formulae, but where we do, it is reasonable to expect something that is consonant with the mimetic element in the action and that takes it a little further.

To sum up, we have, in the upper room, an acknowledged prophetic figure, a moment of intense crisis, a commonplace action, a sense of divine compulsion, the involvement of other people, a material substance, an obvious mimetic element, a verbal formula which deepens rather than explains. Taken together these factors show that the disciples could not have avoided the conclusion that they were involved in a prophetic dramatic act and this would have affected their understanding of what was going on.

If all these similarities have the effect of characterizing the upper room event as prophetic drama, the question is raised whether one other feature of that phenomenon may not be present also. No serious prophetic drama in the Old Testament is self-contained or limited to a small personal or domestic application. Every single one relates to some other greater reality, often on a very large scale. Breaking the pot points to the fall of the city, wearing the yoke means servitude for the whole nation, and so on in every case. However small the action, the fulfilment indicated is grand.

If this is so, we must ask: is there a greater reality to which the drama of the upper room relates? Jesus, as the prophet, is not simply performing an action for his disciples. He is representing a divine activity, of which the upper room is a necessary part, but which goes beyond the upper room into a realm that is akin to the greater realities so easily linked with other prophetic actions. My contention is that the action represents the creation and bonding of a new community that begins in the upper room but that, by repetition, spreads through the whole evangelized world in the form of 'the body of Christ', the church.

How then would the disciples react to Jesus breaking and sharing the bread? If nothing had been done to elevate the action, it would have meant, at the very least, that they were a group of loyal Israelites cementing their bonds of friendship by sharing in common food. But, of course, something *was* done. Some words were spoken – we do not know exactly what – but they identified Jesus with the bread that was broken and shared. In some way it was conveyed to them, 'This is me'. And in interpreting this, we are looking, not for some small personal significance but for meaning on a grand scale. A loaf that is singular is made plural by the breaking, but is then consumed, so that the single loaf is made present in many different people. 'This is my body' means that my*self* is distributed among you to continue my existence and activity in plurality, not simply in the upper room, but on the larger scale, throughout the world and throughout history.

I said a moment ago that, whether it was a Passover or not, the meal would have taken place in the Passover atmosphere. What was that atmosphere and how would it have influenced the way in which the upper room drama was understood and appropriated by the disciples? It was one of both recollection and hope. Israel looked backwards to the great deliverance of the exodus and forwards to the final deliverance of the messianic age. We have to interpret the action of Jesus, therefore, as looking both backwards and forwards, as dramatizing a work of God that was both past and future, and as involving the disciples in a task that had partly been completed but in part lay ahead of them.

4. *The wine*

Now by this time I guess some of you are wondering why I have spent so much time talking about the bread and its meaning without paying any attention to the cup. There is a good reason for this and we had best turn aside to examine it. To us, in our experience of the Lord's Supper, the bread and the wine are completely balanced. We treat them exactly alike. This goes back right to the early Christian communities because both in I Corinthians and Mark, the two earliest witnesses we have, bread and wine occur together. But that does not mean that the phenomenon goes back to the upper room. There is, as I have already said, a vital distinction to be drawn between what we normally regard as the early period, the period of Mark's sources and Paul in the first few decades, and the earl*iest* moment, that is, the upper room itself.

The evidence for the upper room is much more ambiguous about wine and there is one capital difficulty with the idea that wine was used in a way strictly parallel to the bread. It is inconceivable that a gathering of Jews could, completely unprepared, calmly drink wine that was identified with blood. Just as the pre-understanding of the bread meant certain positive things, the pre-understanding of the cup, when once it was linked with blood, meant certain, very powerful, negatives. The whole Jewish cultic system made the drinking of blood anathema. In the course of time, and after a great deal of reflexion, it evidently became possible for wine to be drunk with this connotation, but the wording of the various references in the New Testament make it clear that the idea took a bit of getting used to. Paul, for example, writing to the Corinthians in the fifties does not say, 'This cup is my blood', as he does say, 'This bread is my body'. He says, 'This cup is the new covenant in my blood', showing that the matter still had to be handled with some care. That it could be sprung on the disciples in one jump in the upper room without any warning is very hard, no, impossible to believe.

The earliest name for the eucharist in Luke is 'the breaking of bread', which shows that the bread originally had a certain priority. In the Emmaus story, Jesus took bread, blessed God and broke it, and was thereby known to Cleopas and his companion. No mention of wine. The resurrection meals, which

many link with the eucharistic meals of the early church, are all
about eating and not about drinking. And there is at least one
way of reading the shorter Lukan narrative of the institution
which confines the drama to a single verse relating to the bread.

It is probable that wine came into the Lord's Supper in
different ways in different places and at different speeds. It was
inevitable that it would come in before long. Opposition from
Jewish synagogues and the appearance of Gentile Christians
meant that the Jewish cultic system soon began to lose its grip
on the minds of Christian communities. The Lord's Supper
quickly moved into contexts where drinking wine as blood was
not so problematic and there can be little doubt that the wine
was first thought of as representing blood poured out in sacrifice
rather than blood drunk. Any ritual that was based on eating
would quickly attract a companion based on drinking. And of
course the nearness of the death of Jesus and the ease with
which wine could represent sacrifice made this addition
inevitable and so very positive.

It is not in the least my intention to dispute the place of wine
in the Lord's Supper or to undermine the theology that concentrates on sacrifice. Not at all. The experience of the early
communities and their reflexion is for me a bedrock element of
the New Testament. These ideas were legitimate ways by which
the new community that was coming into being explained itself.
I am simply saying that, in searching for origins, we should not
forget the absolute beginning. We must draw a distinction
between early Mark and Paul and the actual upper room itself,
that is, between a rite in which bread and cup were balanced
and an incident which was simply a breaking of bread. It is a bit
like the question of the origins of the universe. The first few
mini-seconds have an importance of their own, quite apart from
the millions of years that came after.

My point is that the breaking of the bread was not primarily
concerned to interpret Jesus' death. It is concerned with the
whole of his teaching and his mission, and that was focussed in
the founding of a new Israel. In I Cor.11.24 Paul wrote, 'This is
my body which is for you.' But of course the body cannot be

'for you' unless it was in some way pluralized. So participles were inserted, most notably the one we sometimes use, 'this is my body *broken* for you'. The textual evidence suggests that this was not original. But was the person who introduced it anxious to bring the text closer to his idea of violent death, or, equally likely, anxious to stress the new pluralization of the body of Christ? In my view the breaking of the bread did not signify violence at all; it signified pluralization. The bread was broken in order that the body of Christ might be represented, not in the person of the Lord himself, but in the persons of those who believed in him and followed him. We are in touch here with a new medium of the presence of Christ on earth; first in a body of flesh and blood, then in a body of believers. The former, the incarnational body, suffered inevitable limitations; the latter, the body shared by believers, was capable of infinite extension in time and space.

This is the simple and self-evident meaning of the dramatic action. It would require no lengthy explanation. Its meaning would have been obvious immediately to those disciples who were the first recipents. It was a brilliant symbol of corporate being. By the time we get to the Fourth Gospel it has become a symbol of spiritual food, but it is surely obvious that this represents a later reflection. A tiny morsel of bread, not enough to satisfy hunger, is not a good symbol of unlimited spiritual sustenance, but John's usage is simply another example of the way in which the primitive church solved its problems by reinterpreting its sources. It was a perfectly acceptable move by the author of the Fourth Gospel, but he was not as successful in his use of symbols as was Jesus in the upper room, who was simply saying, 'Here I am; now my active presence in the world is to be shared out among yourselves.'

There is a sense in which this action is the natural continuation of the ministry of Jesus. His preaching had been all about the coming of the Kingdom. The Kingdom had drawn near in the ministry of Jesus, but its fullness still waited the final consummation. In the interim there was a period in which the church was the body of Christ, in which the gospel was to be preached to the nations and the way was prepared for the great climax. The upper room then is the beginning of the process whereby the singular body of Christ becomes the multiple presence of Christ in history. And that it still is. Whatever else the Lord's Supper means, it means that we who ingest a particle of the loaf become part of the body which is Christ's visible presence until the end. Whatever else we may believe about Holy Communion, we lose touch with the upper room if we do not believe that.

5. Consequences

This is very much a Methodist gathering and it would be inappropriate if I did not conclude with a few consequential observations directed to the Methodist people. There is much that could be said, but I will confine myself to four points.

In the first place, our celebrations of the Lord's Supper are misleading if we do not begin with a single loaf and plainly break it in the presence of the worshippers. It is commonly supposed that this is impractical, but it isn't. It just requires a little experience and care.

Secondly, instead of worrying about what to do with the pieces left over, we ought to be concerned that nothing is left over. A loaf that represents one person ought to be pluralized and shared so that nothing is left. Again, perfectly practical if we try.

Thirdly, it is evident that we have made far too much of the Lord's Supper as an act of individual piety. Making our communion has become an act of personal, almost private, discipleship. This goes a long way to undermining the fundamental point of the rite. The congregational structure of our larger churches is such that often we find ourselves communicating among people whom we greet somewhat distantly because we hardly know them. But it is as a group that we partake, as a group that we are the body of Christ. What we get out of it individually is a secondary matter.

And fourthly, we must remember that the Lord's Supper has

universal significance. If it heals our private woes, that is fine, but the prophets were not concerned with private woes when they performed their dramas and we must believe that our Lord was not simply enabling Peter and Andrew and James and John to get themselves sorted out in the upper room. In Holy Communion we are sharing in a body that has a universal vocation and that is the measure of the responsibility that we undertake. No doubt we have a problem in working this out in practice, in making the church relevant to this present age, but there is no doubt at all about our vocation to make it so. Receiving the bread means becoming with others the body of Christ on earth, nothing less; sharing the responsibility for making God present among men and women in the modern world as Jesus did within the limits of Galilee.

As I have gone along I have recognized that there are many other interpretations of the Lord's Supper than the one I have argued for here, interpretations that were worked out by the early church in those first creative decades and in the centuries since. None of these has to be surrendered. The boy in the photograph probably grew up to be very different from the child we see there. What he became is as important as what the photograph reveals. But the photograph remains significant and we ought, from time to time, to take a look at it. The origin was like that and it must never be overlooked. My contention is that all the discussion that has gone on about the understanding of the eucharist, both in the New Testament and in later ages, has tended to draw attention away from how things were in the upper room itself. Here I want to remind you of the original occasion, I want to see the original thrust recovered and recognized as significant for our day. I believe that the interpretation of the Last Supper as prophetic drama is one sure way of doing just that.

Bibliography

Texts

Charlesworth, James H., *The Old Testament Pseudepigrapha*, Vol.2, London: Darton, Longman & Todd 1985

Friedlander, Gerald, *Pirkê Rabbi Eliezer*, London: Kegan Paul, Trench & Trubner 1916

Siegert, F., *Drei hellenistisch-jüdische Predigten I*, WUNT 20, Tübingen: Mohr (Siebeck) 1980

—, *Drei hellenistisch-jüdische Predigten II*, WUNT 61, Tübingen: Mohr (Siebeck) 1992

Vermes, Geza, *The Dead Sea Scrolls in English*, London: Penguin, ⁴1995

Josephus (10 vols), Loeb Classical Library, Cambridge MA: Harvard University Press/London: Heinemann 1926–65

Philo (10 vols), Loeb Classical Library, Cambridge MA: Harvard University Press/London: Heinemann 1929–62

Modern authors

Ashton, John, *Studying John: Approaches to the Fourth Gospel*, Oxford: Clarendon Press 1994

—, *Understanding the Fourth Gospel*, Oxford: Clarendon Press 1991

Aune, D.E., *Prophecy in Early Christianity and the Ancient Mediterranean World*, Grand Rapids: Eerdmans 1983

Bacon, B.W., 'What Was the Sign of Jonah?', *BW* 20, 1902, 99–112

Barnett, P.W. 'The Jewish Sign Prophets – A.D. 40–70 – Their Intentions and Origin', *NTS* 27, 1981, 679–97

Barrett, C.K., *The Holy Spirit and the Gospel Tradition*, London: SPCK 1947

Bayer, Hans F., *Jesus' Predictions of Vindication and Resurrection*, WUNT Reihe 2, 20, Tübingen: Mohr (Siebeck) 1986

Barton, John, *Oracles of God*, London: Darton Longman & Todd 1986

Beck, Norman A., 'The Last Supper as an efficacious symbolic act', *JBL* 89, 1970, 192–8

Bentzen, A., *King and Messiah*, Oxford: Blackwell, ET ²1970

Betz, Otto, 'Miracles in the Writings of Flavius Josephus', 212–35 in *Josephus, Judaism and Christianity*, ed. Louis H. Feldman and Gohei Horta, Leiden: Brill 1987

Black, Matthew, *An Aramaic Approach to the Gospels and Acts*, Oxford and New York: OUP ³1967

Boismard, M.-É., *Moses or Jesus*, BETL 84A, Leuven: University Press/ Uitgeverij Peeters, ET 1993

Bowen, C.R., 'Was John the Baptist the Sign of Jonah?', *AJT* 20, 1916, 414–21

Bowker, J.W. 'Prophetic Action and Sacramental Form', in *Studia Evangelica* ed. F.L. Cross, Vol. III, Berlin: Akademie-Verlag 1964, 129–37

Brown, Raymond E., *The Gospel according to John I–XII*, Anchor Bible Commentary, New York: Doubleday 1966

Carmichael, Deborah Bleicher, 'David Daube on the Eucharist and the Passover Seder', *JSNT* 42, 1991, 45–67

Cheyne, 'John the Baptist', *Enc. Biblica* II, 1901, cols. 2498–504

Chow, Simon, *The Sign of Jonah Reconsidered: A Study of its Meaning in the Gospel Traditions*, Coniectanea Biblica New Testament Series 27, Stockholm: Almqvist & Wiksell International 1995

Coakley, J.F., 'Jesus' Messianic Entry into Jerusalem (John 11.11-19)', *JTS* NS 46, 1995, 461–82

Dahood, M., 'The Value of Ugaritic for Textual Criticism', *Biblica* 40, 1959, 160–70

Dalman, G., *Jesus-Joshua*, ET London: SPCK 1929

Dassmann, E., *Sündenvergebung durch Taufe, Busse und Martyrerfürbitte in den Zeugnissen frühchristlicher Frömmigkeit und Kunst*, Münsterische Beiträge zur Theologie 36, Munster: Aschendorff 1973

Daube, David, *He that Cometh*, London Diocesan Council 1966

—, 'The Significance of the Afikoman', in *Pointer*, the Quarterly Journal of the Union of Liberal and Progressive Synagogues, London, Spring 1968, 4f.

—, *Wine in the Bible*, London Diocesan Council 1974

Davies, Paul E., 'Jesus and the Role of the Prophet', *JBL* 64, 1945, 241–54

Derrett, J. Duncan M., 'Law in the New Testament: The Story of the Woman Taken in Adultery', *NTS* 10, 1963, 1–26

Dodd, C. H., 'Jesus as Teacher and Prophet', in *Mysterium Christi*, ed. G.K.A. Bell and Adolf Deissmann, London/New York/Toronto: Longmans, Green and Co. 1930, 53–66

Edwards, Richard A., *The Sign of Jonah*, Studies in Biblical Theology, Series 2, 18, London: SCM Press 1971

Evans, C. F., 'The Central Section of St. Luke's Gospel', in *Studies in the Gospels: Essays in memory of R.H. Lightfoot*, Oxford: Blackwell 1957, 37–53

Evans, Craig A., 'Jesus' Action in the Temple: Cleansing or Portent of Destruction?', *CBQ* 51, 1989, 237–70

Feldman, Louis H., 'Prophets and Prophecy in Josephus', *JTS* NS 41, 1990, 386–422

Fitzmyer, Joseph A., *The Gospel According to Luke X–XXIV*, Anchor Bible Commentary, New York: Doubleday 1983

Fortna, R. T., *The Gospel of Signs*, SNTS Monograph 11, Cambridge: CUP 1970

—, 'Source and Redaction in the Fourth Gospel's Portrayal of Jesus' Signs', *JBL* 89, 1970, 151–66

Fuller, R.H., *The Foundations of New Testament Christology*, London: Lutterworth Press 1965

Gibson, Jeffrey, 'Jesus' Refusal to Produce a "Sign" (Mk 8.11–13)', *JSNT* 38, 1990, 37–66

Glasson, T.F., *Moses in the Fourth Gospel*, Studies in Biblical Theology 40, London: SCM Press 1963

Gordon, R. P. 'From Mari to Moses: Prophecy at Mari and in Ancient Israel', in *Of Prophets' Visions and the Wisdom of Sages*, ed. H. A. McKay and D. J. A. Clines, Sheffield: *JSOT* Supplement 162, 1993, 63–79

Gray, Rebecca, *Prophetic Figures in Late Second Temple Jewish Palestine: The Evidence from Josephus*, Oxford/New York: OUP 1993

Greenspahn, Frederick E., 'Why Prophecy Ceased', *JBL* 108, 1989, 37–49

Hahn, Ferdinand, *The Titles of Jesus in Christology*, London:

Lutterworth Press 1969

Harvey, A. E., *Jesus and the Constraints of History*, London: Duckworth 1982

Hill, David, 'Jesus and Josephus' "Messianic Prophets"', in *Text and Interpretation, Studies in the New Testament Presented to Matthew Black*, ed. Ernest Best and R. McL. Wilson, Cambridge: CUP 1979, 143–54

Hooker, Morna D., 'Beginning from Moses and from all the Prophets', in *From Jesus to John, Essays on Jesus and New Testament Christology in Honour of Marinus de Jonge*, ed. M.C. de Boer, Sheffield: *JSNT* supplement 84, 1993, 216–30

—, *Continuity and Discontinuity*, London: Epworth 1986

—, *The Gospel according to St. Mark*, London: A & C Black 1991

—, 'The Johannine Prologue and the Messianic Secret', *NTS* 21, 1974, 40–58

—, 'Traditions about the Temple in the Sayings of Jesus', *BJRL* 70, 1988, 7–19

—, ' "What Doest Thou Here, Elijah?" A Look at St Mark's Account of the Transfiguration', in *The Glory of Christ in the New Testament: Studies in Christology in Memory of George Bradford Caird*, ed. L. D. Hurst and N. T. Wright, Oxford: Clarendon, 1987, 59–70

Horsley, Richard A., ' "Like One of the Prophets of Old": Two Types of Popular Prophets at the Time of Jesus', *CBQ* 47, 1985, 435–68

—, 'Popular Prophetic Movements at the Time of Jesus: Their Principal Features and Social Origins', *JSNT* 26, 1986, 3–28

Houston, W., 'What Did the Prophets Think They Were Doing? Speech Acts and Prophetic Discourse in the Old Testament', *Biblical Interpretation* 1, 1993, 167–88

Jeremias, J., 'Ἰωνᾶς, *TDNT* III, 406–10

—, *New Testament Theology*, Vol. I, London: SCM Press 1971

—, *The Parables of Jesus*, ET London: SCM Press 1963

—, 'This is My Body . . .', *ExpT* 83, 1972, 196–203

Jonge, M. de, 'Jesus as Prophet and King in the Fourth Gospel', *Analecta Lovaniensia Biblica et Orientalia* V.7, *ETL* XLIX, 1973, 160–77

Kinman, Brent R., *Jesus' Entry into Jerusalem*, AGAJU 28, Leiden, Brill 1995

Kittel, G. and Friedrich, G., *Theological Dictionary of the New*

Testament, ET by G.W. Bromiley, 10 volumes, Grand Rapids: Eerdmans 1964–76 (= *TDNT*)

Leivestad, R., 'Das Dogma von der Prophetenlosen Zeit', *NTS* 19, 1973, 288–99
Linton, O., 'The Demand for a Sign from Heaven', *ST* 19, 1965, 112–29
Lövestam, E., *Jesus and 'This Generation': A New Testament Study*, Coniectanea Biblica New Testament Series 25, Stockholm: Almquist and Wiksell International 1995

Macdonald, J., *The Theology of the Samaritans*, London: SCM Press 1964
Manson, T. W., 'The Pericope de Adultera (Joh 7⁵³—8¹¹)', *ZNW* 44, 1952–3, 255f.
Martyn, J. L., *History and Theology in the Fourth Gospel*, Nashville: Abingdon Press ²1979
Meeks, Wayne A., *The Prophet-King*, NT Supplement 14, Leiden: Brill 1967
Michael, J. H., 'The Sign of John', *JTS* 21, 1919–20, 146–59
Mollat, D., 'Le Semeia Johannique', in *Sacra Pagina* 2, ed. J. Coppens, A. Descamps and E. Massaux, BETL 12–13, Leuven: University Press/ Uitgeverij Peeters 1959
Montgomery, J. A., *The Samaritans*, Philadelphia: John C. Winston 1907
Moxon, C., 'Τὸ σημεῖον Ἰωνα', *ExpT* 22, 1911, 566f.

Neusner, Jacob, 'What "the Rabbis" Thought: A Method and a Result. One Statement on Prophecy in Rabbinic Judaism', in *Pursuing the Text: Studies in Honor of Ben Zion Wacholder on the Occasion of his Seventieth Birthday*, ed. John C. Reeves and John Kampen, JSOT Supplement 184, 1994, 303–20
Nolland, John, *Luke 9:21–18:34*, Word Biblical Commentary, Dallas: Word Books 1993

Overholt, T. W., 'The End of Prophecy: No Players without a Program', *JSOT* 42, 1988, 103–15

Rawlinson, A. E. J., 'Corpus Christi', in *Mysterium Christi*, ed. G. K. A. Bell and Adolf Deissmann, London/New York/Toronto: Longmans,

Green and Co. 1930. 225–44
Robinson, John A. T., *The Body: A Study in Pauline Theology*, Studies in Biblical Theology 5, London: SCM Press 1952

Sanders, E. P., *Jesus and Judaism*, London: SCM Press 1985
—, *The Historical Figure of Jesus*, London: SCM Press 1993
Schmiedel, P. W., 'John, Son of Zebedee', *Enc. Biblica* II, 1901, cols. 2503–62
Schmitt, Götz, 'Das Zeichen des Jona', *ZNTW* 69, 1978, 123–9
Schnackenburg, R., *The Gospel according to St John*, Vol.2, ET London: Burns and Oates 1980
Schweizer, E., σῶμα, *TDNT* VII, 1024–94
Stacey, W. D., *Prophetic Drama in the Old Testament*, London: Epworth Press 1990
—, (David), *Isaiah 1–39*, London: Epworth Press 1993
—, (David), 'The Lord's Supper as Prophetic Drama: The A.S. Peake Lecture for 1993', *Epworth Review* 21, January 1994, 65–74
Stanton, Graham N., 'Jesus of Nazareth: A Magician and a False Prophet Who Deceived God's People?', in *Jesus of Nazareth Lord and Christ*, ed. J.B. Green and M. Turner (*FS* I.H. Marshall), Grand Rapids: Eerdmans 1994
Stuiber, A., *Refrigerium Interim: Die Vorstellungen vom Zwischen-zustand und die frühchristliche Grabeskunst*, Theophaneia 11, Bonn: Peter Hanstein 1957
Swetnam, J., 'Some Signs of Jonah', *Biblica* 68, 1987, 74–9

Teeple, Howard M., *The Mosaic Eschatological Prophet*, *JBL* Monograph 10, 1957
Telford, William, *The Barren Temple and the Withered Tree*, *JSNT* Supplement 1, Sheffield 1980
Thiselton, Anthony C., 'The Supposed Power of Words in the Biblical Writings', *JTS* NS 25, 1974, 283–99

Vermes, G., *Jesus the Jew*, London: Collins 1973
—, *The Religion of Jesus the Jew*, London: SCM Press 1993
Viberg, Åke, *Symbols of Law: A Contextual Analysis of Legal Symbolic Acts in the Old Testament*, Coniectanea Biblica Old Testament Series 34, Stockholm: Almqvist & Wiksell International 1992

Weeden, T., *Mark – Traditions in Conflict*, Philadelphia: Fortress Press

1971

Wright, N. T., *The New Testament and the People of God*, London: SPCK 1992

Young, Franklin W., 'Jesus the Prophet: A Re-examination', *JBL* 68, 1948, 285–99

Notes

Full publication details of works cited in the notes are given in the Bibliography

I. 'Is This Not the Prophet?'

1. See, e.g., J. W. Bowker, 'Prophetic Action and Sacramental Form'.
2. See, in particular, A. E. Harvey, who discusses the significance of some of Jesus' prophetic actions, *Jesus and the Constraints of History*, 57–62, 120–53. It is significant that E. P. Sanders begins his discussion of Jesus from the tradition about what he *did*, rather than what he *said*: *Jesus and Judaism*, 1–13.
3. W. D. Stacey, *Prophetic Drama in the Old Testament*.
4. David Stacey, 'The Lord's Supper as Prophetic Drama'.
5. The *hithpa'el* of the Hebrew verb *nb'*, to 'prophesy', refers to action or behaviour, usually of a frenzied kind. Cf. I Sam. 10.5ff.; 19.20ff.; 18.10.
6. Cf. Hos. 12.13: 'By a prophet the Lord brought Israel up from Egypt, and by a prophet Israel was tended.'
7. I Sam. 3.20.
8. An even more bizarre action is recorded of a prophet at Mari, in the eighteenth century BC (Text 206). He is said to have devoured a raw lamb and announced a devouring that threatened the nation. See R. P. Gordon, 'From Mari to Moses: Prophecy at Mari and in Ancient Israel', 69.
9. Isa. 20.
10. Jer. 19.
11. Ezek. 2.9–3.3.
12. Ezek. 4.4–6.
13. Ex. 14.10–31.
14. I Kings 17.17–24.
15. II Kings 5.1–19.
16. Isa. 20.4.
17. Jer. 19.11.
18. Hos. 1.2–8.
19. Contrast the popular explanation of prophetic actions as given by

J. W. Bowker, 'Prophetic Action and Sacramental Form', 130: 'A prophetic action is the realistic release of the energy of God, it is the irreversible setting in motion of His activity. It is as though I kicked a football towards a window: nothing can avert the catastrophe: I might just as well say that the window is already broken. And yet I still do have to wait for the actual crash of broken glass . . . Thus a prophetic act is not a prediction, it is the release of an inevitable circumstance which nothing can avert.'

20. Cf. Anthony Thiselton's discussion of the 'power' of the word in 'The Supposed Power of Words in the Biblical Writings'. He attacks the idea that belief in the potency of God's word was based on some kind of 'word magic' whereby *all* words had power; God's word was potent because it had its origin with God and was spoken with his authority. See in particular Isa. 55.6–11. Cf. also W. Houston, 'What Did the Prophets Think They Were Doing? Speech Acts and Prophetic Discourse in the Old Testament'.

21. There are interesting examples of God himself 'repenting' of his plan to destroy, cf. Amos 7.1–6 (a prophetic vision), Jonah 3.1–10 (an oracle); Jer. 18.1–8 (a dramatic sign).

22. W. D. Stacey, *Prophetic Drama in the Old Testament*, 260–82.

23. Ex. 14.13.

24. Ex. 4.1–9.

25. Judg. 6.17–22.

26. I Kings 18.30–39.

27. II Kings 20.5–11.

28. I Sam. 10.1–9.

29. Isa. 7.10–17. See David Stacey, *Isaiah 1–39*, 55–7.

30. We are not dealing here with omens which occur and which are subsequently interpreted by a prophet.

31. Deut. 18.15–22.

32. The exception is Isa. 7.10–17, where the sign offered to Ahaz is itself a symbol of the salvation of Israel. The birth, naming and growth of the child are in fact treated as though they were a prophetic drama, even though the prophet takes no action – unless, as is possible, the child is his own. See W.D. Stacey, *Prophetic Drama in the Old Testament*, 116–20.

33. I Macc. 9.27.

34. I Macc. 14.41.

35. *Apion* 1.41.

36. See R. Leivestad, 'Das Dogma von der Prophetenlosen Zeit'; A. E. Harvey, *Jesus and the Constraints of History*, 58f.; John Barton, *Oracles of God*, 105–16; Thomas W. Overholt, 'The End of Prophecy: No Players without a Program'; Rebecca Gray, *Prophetic Figures in Late Second Temple Jewish Palestine: The Evidence from Josephus*, 7–34; Jacob Neusner, 'What "the Rabbis" Thought: A Method and a Result. One Statement on Prophecy in Rabbinic Judaism'; Frederick E. Greenspahn, 'Why Prophecy Ceased'. Louis H. Feldman, on the other hand, in 'Prophets and Prophecy in Josephus', continues to argue that Josephus considered prophecy to have ceased, though he agrees that this was a minority opinion, not the popular view.
37. So, too, Philo, *De Spec. Leg.* 1.65.
38. The exceptions to the rule serve only to prove the point. Josephus himself refers to figures among the Essenes whom we might term 'prophets', but he uses the word *mantis* of them, rather than *prophētēs*. The teacher at Qumran was perhaps a prophetic figure, but we know almost nothing about him. Anna, who greets the infant Jesus in the Temple, is described by Luke as a prophetess (Luke 2.36–38); since Anna's welcome parallels that of Simeon, Luke probably thought of him also as a prophet. Since Luke associated the birth of Jesus with the activity of the Holy Spirit, it was natural for him to describe one of those inspired by the Spirit as a prophetess. Mary (or Elizabeth, according to some Latin mss. and a few patristic writers) and Zechariah exercise a similar prophetic role when they burst into hymns of praise.
39. I QS 9.11.
40. We should perhaps add John 7.52, where P66 and P75 both read *ho prophētēs*. Raymond Brown accepts this as the original reading (*The Gospel according to John I–XII*, 325).
41. IV Q 175.
42. This passage seems to have referred originally to the succession of prophets after Moses, but eventually came to be understood of the eschatological prophet.
43. For a discussion of the Fourth Evangelist's use of these ideas in relation to the beliefs of his Jewish contemporaries, see J. L. Martyn, *History and Theology in the Fourth Gospel*, 102–28.
44. Cf. J. A. Montgomery, *The Samaritans*, 243–50; J. Macdonald, *The Theology of the Samaritans*, 359–71.
45. Some scholars have suggested that the description of the Servant

in Deutero-Isaiah has been influenced by the hope for a prophet like Moses. See, e.g., A. Bentzen, *King and Messiah*, 65–7. The call of Jeremiah in Jer. 1.7, 9 appears to be modelled on Deut. 18.18, but since the date of Deut. 18.15–18 is uncertain, the influence could be in the opposite direction.

46. Mark 9.11–13//Matt. 17.10–12; Matt. 11.14. Cf. Luke 1.17. In Mark 15.35f. //Matt. 27.47–49, Elijah is seen as one who comes to help those in need, and who might therefore come to save Jesus. There is irony here: in both Mark and Matthew, Elijah is said to have come already, in the person of John, and has himself been put to death.

47. John 1.21,25. In both verses, Elijah is clearly differentiated from 'the prophet'.

48. Mark 6.14f.//Luke 9.7f.; Mark 8.27f.//Matt. 16.13f.//Luke 9.18f.

49. For the variety of expectation, see also Howard M. Teeple, *The Mosaic Eschatological Prophet*.

50. II Kings 1.8.

51. Matt. 3.9//Luke 3.8.

52. John 1.25f., 28, 31, 33; 3.23; 4.1; 10.40.

53. This is consistent with the rest of the Fourth Gospel, since – with the exception of 20.23 – there is no reference to repentance or forgiveness as such anywhere.

54. John 1.6–9,15,19–34; 3.25–30; 5.33–55.

55. *Antt.* 18.116–9.

56. John 1.26f.

57. The phrase he uses is *baptismōi sunienai*.

58. I QS 3. Cf. also I QS 4: 'He will cleanse him of all wicked deeds with the spirit of holiness; like purifying waters He will shed upon him the spirit of truth (to cleanse him) of all abomination and injustice. And he shall be plunged into the spirit of purification that he may instruct the upright in the knowledge of the Most High and teach the wisdom of the sons of heaven to the perfect of way. For God has chosen them for an everlasting Covenant and all the glory of Adam shall be theirs.'

59. Isa. 1.16f.

60. Ps. 51.7, 9f.

61. Ezek. 36.24–27.

62. In John 10.41 we are told that the crowds remarked that 'John gave us no sign'. Is this an ironic comment by the evangelist, or did he reserve the term *sēmeion* for Jesus' actions? Since John's

baptism is mentioned only in passing (see n.52, above), the latter seems the more likely explanation. For further discussion, see Chapter 4, n.42, below, 118.

63. Mark 1.5; Matt. 3.5.
64. Fire can purge as well as destroy. See Isa. 4.4; Mal. 3.2. Both passages mix the metaphors of washing and purging.
65. Cf. Acts 2.38; 8.15–17; 10.47; 19.1–6; I Cor. 6.11; 12.13; Titus 3.5f.; John 3.5.
66. The label appears to have been coined by P. W. Barnett: see 'The Jewish Sign Prophets – A.D. 40–70 – Their Intentions and Origin'.
67. Among the terms he uses are *goēs, pseudoprophētēs, planoi* and *apateōnes.*
68. *Antt.* 20.97–99.
69. *Antt.* 20.169–72. A somewhat different account is given in *War* 2.261–63.
70. *Antt.* 20.168; *War* 2.258–60.
71. *War* 6.283–87.
72. *War* 7.437–41.
73. Cf. the reference to false prophets who do signs and wonders in order to deceive, Matt. 24.24//Mark 13.22. The 'sign prophets' are all later than Jesus, but it is possible that the evangelists had some of them in mind at this point.
74. Rebecca Gray, *Prophetic Figures in Late Second Temple Jewish Palestine*, 112–44.
75. The one possible exception to this occurs in *Antt.* 2.327, and is ambiguous.
76. *Antt.* 2.274, 276, 280, 283, 284.
77. A similar distinction is made by O. Betz, 'Miracles in the Writings of Flavius Josephus', 223f.
78. Deut. 18.22.
79. Matt. 16.14//Mark 8.28//Luke 9.19; Luke 9.7f.
80. Mark 6.15. Luke 9.7f. does not agree with Mark here.
81. Cf. Matt. 21.46.
82. Cf. Matt. 26.68//Luke 22.64.
83. Cf. John 4.44.
84. John 4.19; 9.17. The suggestion is dismissed by the religious authorities in 7.52.
85. John 6.14; 7.40. According to P66 and P75, which read the article before the noun, it is this belief which is dismissed in 7.52.
86. Acts 3.22; 7.37.

87. B. Sanh. 43a. G. N. Stanton has recently discussed other early evidence that Jesus was seen as a magician and false prophet or deceiver. In addition to the rabbinic material, he looks at Christian evidence from Justin Martyr, the Acts of Thomas and elsewhere. He reassesses the passage about Jesus in Josephus (*Antt.* 18.63–64), and judges it to be basically hostile. He argues that the evidence of widespread allegations in the second and third century AD that Jesus was a sorcerer and a false prophet who deceived the people suggests that the charges have their origin in the lifetime of Jesus himself. See Graham N. Stanton, 'Jesus of Nazareth: A Magician and a False Prophet Who Deceived God's People?'.

88. 'Jesus as Teacher and Prophet'.

II. 'No Sign Shall be Given Them'

1. Luke perhaps knows both stories, since the language he uses of the request, in 11.16, echoes that used in the *other* story, at Matt. 16.1 and Mark 8.11.

2. Matt. 16.1; Mark 8.11; Luke 11.16.

3. Matt. 24.24//Mark 13.22. The longer ending of Mark uses the word twice in a positive sense, to refer to miracles performed by the apostles which lead men and women to believe (Mark 16.17, 20).

4. Cf. Herod's expectation that Jesus would do some sign, Luke 23.8. Attestation by miracles was required of prophets (Deut. 13.1–5), but not of rabbis. See F. Hahn, *The Titles of Jesus in Christology*, 378f.

5. The comment in Deut. 34.10–12 which says that there has never been another prophet like Moses goes on to explain that he has been unequalled for signs and wonders.

6. John 6.30. Cf. 4.48.

7. The noun *sēmeion* is used relatively frequently in this sense in the Old Testament and in Acts, and occasionally elsewhere. Cf. Deut. 6.22; 7.19; 26.8; Jer. 32(LXX 39).21; Acts 2.43; 14.3; 15.12; Rom. 15.19; II Cor. 12.12; Heb. 2.4.

8. Since the reference to the sign of Jonah is found only in Matthew and Luke, it has been argued that it originated in the 'Q-community'. See R. A. Edwards, *The Sign of Jonah*, 83–7. Cf. also G. Schmitt, 'Das Zeichen des Jona', who regards Mark 8.11

as the earliest form of the saying. S. Chow, *The Sign of Jonah Reconsidered*, does not even discuss the possibility that the phrase goes back to Jesus! The fact that Matthew and Luke give different explanations suggests that the phrase belongs to an early stage of the tradition. If it does not go back to Jesus himself, we still have to explain its original meaning and why it was added to the outright refusal to give a sign in Mark. The alternative explanation is that Mark (or the tradition before him) was baffled by the phrase, and therefore dropped it.

9. J. Jeremias, "Ἰωνᾶς", 409, argued that Luke's interpretation is similar to Matthew's, since for Luke, 'the *tertium comparationis* is that Jonah became a sign to the Ninevites, obviously as one who had been delivered from the belly of the fish, and that Jesus will be displayed to this generation as the One who is raised up from the dead. According to Lk, then, both the old and the new sign of Jonah consist in the authorization of the divine messenger by deliverance from death.' Jeremias admits that we are not in fact told that the Ninevites were ever told of Jonah's rescue, which makes his claim that this interpretation was 'obvious' somewhat dubious; he also ignores the fact that Luke nowhere suggests that Jesus is 'displayed to his generation as the One who is raised up from the dead'! On the contrary, Jesus appears only to his disciples, and reports of his resurrection are denied by the authorities.

10. According to II Kings 14.25, he came from Gath-hepher.

11. John 7.52, cf. v.41.

12. Although that, of course, does not exclude it from consideration, since whatever Jesus is offering is unlikely to be a sign of that kind.

13. Matt. 12.41//Luke 11.32.

14. Luke 13.6–9. Matt. 21.18–22//Mark 11.12–14, 20–24.

15. J. Swetnam, 'Some Signs of Jonah', argues that in Matthew the sign is not Jonah himself but his prophecy. This seems an unlikely interpretation of the term *sēmeion*. For Swetnam, the reference to Jonah's sojourn in the belly of the sea-monster is the justification for the comparison between Jesus' prophecy and Jonah's.

16. Matt. 12.25–29; Luke 11.17–22.

17. E.g. the much later *Gen. Rab.* xviii.11 and *Pirkê Rabbi Eliezer* 33.

18. I Kings 17.8–24. *Lives* 10.6 links the boy's death and restoration to life with his (i.e. Jonah's) attempt to run away from God (Jonah

1.3) and his subsequent escape from the fish (*Lives* 10.2).

19. Translation by D.R.A. Hare, in *The Old Testament Pseud-epigrapha*, Vol.2, ed. James H. Charlesworth, 379–99. The idea that Jonah prophesied against his own people is found also in *Pirkê Rabbi Eliezer* 10.

20. F. Siegert, *Drei hellenistisch-jüdische Predigten*, 25, translates the Armenian *kerparan* by *Wahrzeichen* and *Sinnbild*.

21. For this, cf. *Mek.* on Ex. 12.1, which explains Jonah's reluctance to go to Nineveh as due to his fear that the Gentiles were more likely than his own people to repent, and that Israel would thus be condemned. *Lam. Rab. Proems* 31 (8b) also contrasts the one prophet whom God sent to Nineveh, who repented, with the many sent to Jerusalem, who met with no response.

22. Mark 13.4//Luke 21.7. Cf. Matt. 24.3.

23. Matthew indicates this in his version of the question: 'When will these things happen? And what will be the sign of your coming and the end of the age?' (Matt. 24.3).

24. Matt. 24.15//Mark 13.14; Luke 21.20,24.

25. Matt. 24.29–31; Mark 13.24–27; Luke 21.25–28.

26. Matt. 27.45//Mark 15.33//Luke 23.44.

27. Matt. 27.51//Mark 15.38//Luke 23.45.

28. Matt. 27.52f.

29. So, e.g., B.W. Bacon, 'What Was the Sign of Jonah?'

30. Matt. 21.25//Mark 11.30//Luke 20.4. The demand in Matt. 16.1, Mark 8.11 and Luke 11.16 is for a sign 'from heaven'. O. Linton, 'The Demand for a Sign from Heaven', 116–18, argues that these words are due to Markan redaction, and that the original demand was simply for 'a sign'. He may be right, but the demand is in any case for divine authentication, and in *that* sense, for a sign from heaven; it is not necessarily a request for the kind of sign described in Mark 13, as is argued by Jeffrey Gibson, in 'Jesus' Refusal to Produce a "Sign" (Mk 8.11–13)'.

31. It was the difficulty of seeing how Jonah could be a sign to 'this generation' that led C. Moxon, 'τὸ σημεῖον 'Ιωνα', to argue that the saying in Matt. 12.39//Luke 11.29 referred to 'the sign of John'.

32. For the similarities in the names, see T.K. Cheyne, 'John the Baptist', col. 2502; P.W. Schmiedel, 'John, Son of Zebedee', col. 2505.

33. Cf. John 1.42 and 21.15–17, where the mss vary between 'Jonah'

(as in Matt. 16.17) and 'John'.

34. Cf. J.H. Michael, 'The Sign of John'.

35. E.g. Irenaeus, *Contra Haereses* 3.20.1–2; Clement, *Stromata* 1.21; Origen, *Comm. in Mt.* 16.1–4.

36. Cf. Simon Chow, *The Sign of Jonah Reconsidered*, 175–210.

37. What *is* perhaps surprising if this suggestion is right is the fact that none of the Church Fathers links the sign of Jonah with baptism. There is, however, some evidence that the story of Jonah was associated with baptism in artistic representations of the second and third centuries AD. It is, e.g., found in connection with the theme of baptism in room 5 of the catacombs at SS Pietro e Marcellino in Rome; see E. Dassmann, *Sündenvergebung durch Taufe, Busse und Martyrerfürbitte*, 363ff. Dassmann argues that Jonah was closely associated with the theme of repentance and forgiveness, see 222–32, 356–72, 385–97. Jonah appears in more early Christian artefacts than any other figure. Most common is the representation of Jonah at rest under the gourd. The three-part cycle of Jonah (Jonah being thrown into the sea from the ship and into the jaws of the sea-monster; Jonah being spewed out on to dry land; Jonah at rest under the gourd) is common. The cycle seems to be an allusion to death, resurrection and heavenly bliss, though some writers have interpreted the final scene as a reference to an interim state (see A Stuiber, *Refrigerium Interim*, 136–51). Fundamental to all these representations of Jonah is the idea that he was delivered by God from judgment and destruction. Why was the Jonah cycle so popular in early Christian art? On sarcophagi, the Jonah cycle seems to be an obvious depiction of the Christian hope of resurrection (see S. Chow, *The Sign of Jonah Reconsidered*, 194–209). But was its popularity also due to the fact that (like the story of Noah) it was seen as a symbol of baptism?

38. Matthew has these sayings elsewhere in 7.7–11, but reads *agatha* (good things) for *pneuma hagion*.

39. Commentators have usually argued that Luke's 'the finger of God' is more original than Matthew's 'the Spirit of God', but J. Nolland, *Luke 9:21–18:34*, 639f., points out that recent studies of the question have all supported Matthew's version. The meaning, in any case, is the same, since both phrases refer to God's creative activity.

40. Matt. 21.23–27//Mark 11.27–33//Luke 20.1–8.

41. Matt. 3.2; Mark 1.4//Luke 3.3.
42. Mark 1.4//Luke 3.3. In Matt. 3.6 those whom he baptizes confess their sins.
43. Cf. E. Lövestam, *Jesus and 'This Generation'*, 32.
44. The general meaning is the same, even if we assume that the neuter *pleion* refers to John and Jesus themselves, rather than to what they did.
45. Similarly B. W. Bacon, 'What Was the Sign of Jonah?', 109, who interprets the saying as a reference to John's call to repentance and Jesus' message of forgiveness.
46. Matt. 11.18f.//Luke 7.33f. The parallel is noted by B. W. Bacon, loc. cit.
47. Cf. Luke 11.49. See also J. Fitzmyer's comment on Luke 11.31: 'The phraseology recalls that of 7:35. God's wisdom is vindicated by the judgment that will be passed, not on Jesus by his genera-tion, but on it by those who accept him and so prove to be "her [wisdom's] children"' (*The Gospel According to Luke X–XXIV*, 937).
48. Matt. 11.2–6.
49. The saying in Matt. 12.41f.//Luke 11.31f. is about hearing wis-dom, but the context concerns works of exorcism.
50. Cf. J. H. Michael, 'The Sign of John', 155, who remarks that 'in almost every instance when Jesus speaks of John the implication is present that if his hearers had known the Baptist they would have recognized Him also'. The significance of this link has been entirely missed by C. R. Bowen, 'Was John the Baptist the Sign of Jonah?', who answers his question in the negative, arguing that 'The demand brought to Jesus is that *he* should show some sign that would serve as *his* legitimation . . . The sign must come from him, or be something directly related to himself . . . However true it is to say that John the Baptist was a sign to his generation that the end of all things was at hand, it is quite meaningless for Jesus to point to him as a sign of the validity of his own message' (421). Bowen makes no reference to Jesus' reply to the challenge in the temple!
51. Matt. 11.14.
52. John 1.19–36.
53. Matt. 21.23–27//Mark 11.27–33//Luke 20.1–8.
54. Matt. 4.2; Luke 4.2.
55. Matt. 16.1; Mark 8.11; Luke 11.16.

56. Ex. 17.1–7.
57. Cf. I Cor.10.1–13, where a similar double meaning is found: Paul describes the incident at Massah when the people tested the Lord as a warning to Christians not to do the same, and concludes by saying that the Corinthians have not yet had to face up to a *peirasmos* which is beyond their endurance and that God can be trusted not to allow them to be tested beyond their power (v.13).
58. Matt. 21.23//Mark 11.28//Luke 20.2.
59. Matt. 9.1–8//Mark 2.1–12//Luke 5.17–26.
60. Matt. 11.4–6, Luke 7.21–23.
61. Jeffrey Gibson, 'Jesus' Refusal to Produce a "Sign" (Mk 8.11–13)', fails to make this distinction (40–2) and ignores the fact that Mark does not use the term *sēmeion* in chapter 2. By doing so he refuses (to use his own words!) 'to allow both the story and Mark to speak in their own terms'.

III. *'The Signs of a Prophet'*

1. Matt. 14.33.
2. E. P. Sanders, *Jesus and Judaism*, 11.
3. Matt. 11.4f.//Luke 7.22.
4. Matt. 12.25–29//Luke 11.17–22; cf. Mark 3.23–27.
5. Matt. 12.38–42; Luke 11.29–32.
6. Matt. 15.21–28//Mark 7.24–30.
7. Contrast Matt. 13.54–58//Mark 6.1–6.
8. Matt. 8.5–13//Luke 7.1–10; cf. John 4.46–54.
9. Mark 5.1–20//Luke 8.26–39. Matthew's story, in Matt. 8.28–34, is about two men, though it is much shorter, and lacks much of the detail in Mark and Luke.
10. E. P. Sanders, *Jesus and Judaism*, 101.
11. J. Jeremias, *New Testament Theology*, Vol. I, 235.
12. Matt.19.28//Luke 22.28–30.
13. Mark and Luke refer to this when they list the disciples (Mark 3.16; Luke 6.14); Matthew links the renaming with Caesarea Philippi (Matt. 16.18), and John associates it with Jesus' first meeting with Peter (John 1.42).
14. Mark tells us that Jesus also gave the name 'Boanerges', 'sons of thunder', to the sons of Zebedee, Mark 3.17. The significance of this is unfortunately obscure.
15. Hos.1.3–9; Isa. 8.1–4.

16. So Matt. 9.13//Mark 2.17. The verb *kaleō* means 'to invite', but this sense has been lost in Luke's version, since he has added the words *eis metanoian* (Luke 5.32).
17. Luke 19.1–10.
18. Matt. 9.14//Mark 2.18//Luke 5.33.
19. Matt. 12.2//Mark 2.24//Luke 6.2.
20. Matt. 15.2//Mark 7.5.
21. A good example is found in Jeremiah's use of the Rechabites in Jer. 35.
22. John 21.1–14.
23. Matt. 10.14f.//Mark 6.11//Luke 9.5; cf. Luke 10.11f.
24. Matt. 18.1–5; Mark 9.35–37//Luke 9.47f.
25. Mark 10.13–16//Luke 18.15–17; contrast Matt. 19.13–15.
26. *An Aramaic Approach to the Gospels and Acts*, 218–23.
27. Matt. 21.1–9//Mark 11.1–10//Luke 19.28–38; cf. John 12.12–16.
28. Cf. A. E. Harvey, J*esus and the Constraints of History*, 121.
29. See B.R. Kinman, *Jesus' Entry into Jerusalem*, 49–54, 109–113, who examines the relevance of this incident for the story as it is told in Luke.
30. I am not persuaded by J. F. Coakley's recent argument (based on John and Luke) that Jesus rode the donkey unwillingly. See 'Jesus' Messianic Entry into Jerusalem'.
31. Matt. 21.18–22//Mark 11.12–14, 20–24.
32. Luke 13.6–9.
33. See, for both these points, William Telford, *The Barren Temple and the Withered Tree*.
34. Matt. 21.12f.//Mark 11.15–17//Luke 19.45f. Cf. John 2.13–17.
35. Matt. 21.28–22.10.
36. Luke 19.41–44.
37. John 2.19.
38. E.P. Sanders, *Jesus and Judaism*, 61; italics mine.
39. Nevertheless, the *way* in which these things were administered was open to corruption. For a very different assessment from Sanders', see Craig A. Evans, 'Jesus' Action in the Temple'. Evans points to evidence of criticism of the priesthood.
40. *Jesus and Judaism*, 75.
41. 'Traditions about the Temple in the Sayings of Jesus', 7–19.
42. In addition to the story of the fig tree, see the parable of the vineyard in Matt. 21.33–46//Mark 12.1–12//Luke 20.9–19.

43. Matt. 22.34–40//Mark 12.28–34.
44. Matt. 23.1–36//Mark 12.38–40//Luke 20.45–47.
45. Matt. 23.37–39//Luke 13.34f. Cf. Luke 19.41–44.
46. See espec. Jer. 7.1–15; v.11 is quoted in all three Synoptic Gospels at this point. Cf. Micah 3.9–12.
47. 'Traditions about the Temple in the Sayings of Jesus'; *The Gospel according to St. Mark*, 261–6.
48. Cf. my husband's comment: some prophetic dramas, he wrote, 'take place in circumstances where repentance is still possible and fulfilment not inevitable' (W. D. Stacey, *Prophetic Drama in the Old Testament*, 275). See Jer. 18.8: if the nation repents, God may spare it; Jer. 27: the nation can refuse to submit to the yoke of Babylon – though it will be destroyed if it does refuse.
49. John 2.16. See below, n.52
50. M. Berakoth 9.5.
51. Mark 12.28–34; cf. Matt. 22.34–40; Luke 10.25–28.
52. Amos 5.21f., 24.
53. Cf. John 2.16, where Jesus demands that the traders should not make his Father's house into a house 'of market'.
54. David Stacey, 'The Lord's Supper as Prophetic Drama'. Cf. Norman A. Beck, 'The Last Supper as an Efficacious Symbolic Act'. The difference in approach is epitomized in the language chosen by each author for his title – 'prophetic drama' and 'efficacious symbolic act'. Throughout his article, Beck assumed that prophetic actions were 'efficacious symbolic acts'; he distinguished them (correctly) from 'parabolic actions', or mere illustrations, but (following Wheeler Robinson and Fohrer), supposed them to have been actions 'initiating divine activity'. This is precisely the point disputed by my husband, who argued that prophetic actions were neither 'parabolic' nor 'efficacious', but 'dramas' representing the divine will.
55. Jer. 19.
56. See the discussion in G. Dalman, *Jesus-Joshua*, 142f., though he rejects that interpretation in this context. Cf. J. A. T. Robinson, *The Body*, 11–16; E. Schweizer, 'σῶμα', *TDNT* VII, 1971, 1059.
57. David Daube, *He that Cometh*; 'The Significance of the Afikoman'; *Wine in the Bible*.
58. Deborah Carmichael, 'David Daube on the Eucharist and the Passover Seder'.
59. It is, of course, by no means certain that the Last Supper *was* a

Passover meal. I believe that the evidence favours the Johannine dating.

60. Luke 24.35.

61. Acts 2.42, 46; 20.7, 11. It is often assumed that these passages refer to some kind of *agape*, rather than the Lord's Supper. Whatever the nature of the meal, the act of breaking the bread had clearly taken on a new significance.

62. I Cor. 10.16.

63. I Kings 19.19–21.

64. Matt. 26.20; Mark 14.10; Luke 22.14 'the apostles'; cf. Luke 22.30, where Jesus 'covenants a kingdom' to the disciples. They are to share his authority by judging the twelve tribes of Israel. John 6.67 also links the Twelve with the eucharistic tradition; cf. possibly v.13.

65. Matt.26.23//Mark 14.20. Cf. John 13.26.

66. Matt. 26.27//Mark 14.23. Cf. Luke 22.20.

67. The argument is parallel to the one Paul used a few chapters earlier, in 6.12–20. There, he argued that those who are members of Christ should not be joined in sexual union to prostitutes: it is impossible to be members of Christ and members of a prostitute at the same time.

68. E.g. by A. E. J. Rawlinson, 'Corpus Christi'.

69. E.g. by J. A. T. Robinson, *The Body*, 57.

70. Luke 22.17.

71. Matt. 26.29//Mark 14.25.

72. Luke 22.18.

73. Luke 22.29f.

74. Wine is a symbol of blessing, Gen. 27.28, and thus of future restoration and the messianic kingdom; see Isa. 25.6; Amos 9.13f.; Hos. 2.22; Joel 2.24–26; 3.18; II Bar. 29.5; I Enoch 10.19.

75. Cf. also I QS 6, which describes the meal of the covenant community preparing for the last days.

76. Is the saying in Luke 22.29f. the origin of this development? Certainly it is significant that Jesus' words about passing on his authority to his disciples ('covenanting a kingdom') are found in the context of the Last Supper.

77. Ex. 24.8.

78. In Hebrew thought, the blood of the animal killed in a sacrifice represented its life. See Lev. 17.11.

79. Cf. Lev. 17.10–14.

80. See Gen. 26.26–31; 31.43–54; II Sam. 3.17–30. Cf. Åke Viberg, *Symbols of Law*, 70–6.

IV. 'More than a Prophet'

1. It is unnecessary to discuss here *who* the authors of our four Gospels were. For the sake of convenience, I refer to the authors by the names attributed to the Gospels by tradition.
2. T. Weeden, *Mark – Traditions in Conflict*.
3. Mark 4.41. Cf. Matt. 8.27 and Luke 8.25.
4. The first comes in 8.22–26, immediately after a story about the incomprehension of the disciples, and immediately before Caesarea Philippi. The second comes in 10.46–52, at the end of the section in which Jesus has been teaching his disciples what following him means, and in which the disciples have repeatedly shown their inability to comprehend. Matthew and Luke omit the first story.
5. Mark 7.31–37. Contrast 4.12.
6. See M. D. Hooker, 'What Doest Thou Here, Elijah?'.
7. Mark 14.3–9. Cf. Matt. 26.6–13.
8. Luke 7.36–50; John 12.1–8.
9. Mark 14.63. Cf. Matt. 26.65.
10. Cf. Matt. 27.51. Luke (23.45) records the omen, but not the high priest's action.
11. Mark 15.16–19. Cf. Matt. 27.27–30. In Luke (23.11), it is Herod and his soldiers who mock Jesus.
12. Mark 15.26. Cf. Matt. 27.37; Luke 23.38.
13. Mark 15.30–32//Matt. 27.42. Cf. Luke 23.35–37. There are similar examples of prophetic 'inactions' serving as prophetic drama in the Old Testament: Jeremiah does not marry, mourn or feast (16.1–9); Ezekiel does not mourn his wife (24.15–24).
14. Matt. 1.21,25.
15. Whether the blind and lame were in fact ever excluded from the temple is not clear, but the Qumran texts contain several references to the fact that people with physical infirmities were to be excluded from the *congregation*. See I QSa 2.5–7; I QM 7.4–5.
16. Matt. 8.16f.
17. Matt. 11.2–6. Isa. 29.18; 35.5f.; 42.7,18; 26.19; 61.1.
18. Matt. 16.1–20.
19. Matt. 2.16–21.

20. Luke 1.59–66; 2.21.
21. Luke 1.68–79. Zechariah behaves here like a prophet, and is said to be filled with the Holy Spirit. Cf. Chapter 1, n.38. Like Ezekiel (3.22–27; 24.25–27; 33.21f.), he was struck dumb, though this was the result of his own refusal to believe the divine message, not as a sign of the refusal of others to hear it.
22. Luke 1.46–55.
23. Luke 4.16–30.
24. Luke 7.11–17; I Kings 17.17–24; II Kings 4.32–37.
25. Luke 7.18–23. Cf. Matt. 11.2–6.
26. Luke 9.59–62.
27. Elisha was ploughing – cf. Luke 9.62; he wanted to say goodbye to his parents – cf. Luke 9.59, 61.
28. Matt.17.9–13//Mark 9.9–13.
29. C.F. Evans, 'The Central Section of St. Luke's Gospel'.
30. See Morna D. Hooker, 'Beginning from Moses and from all the Prophets'.
31. Chapter I, 7f., 15.
32. John 8.28; 12.49; 14.10. Cf. Deut. 18.18.
33. John 1.45.
34. Morna D. Hooker, 'The Johannine Prologue and the Messianic Secret', 53–8.
35. For the importance of the figure of Moses, see T.F. Glasson, *Moses in the Fourth Gospel*; Morna D. Hooker, *Continuity and Discontinuity*, 68–71; John Ashton, *Understanding the Fourth Gospel*, 470–6; M.É. Boismard, *Moses or Jesus*.
36. John 5.39, 45–47.
37. See Chapter II, 32f.
38. The exception is 2.18, which is not an exception since, as we have seen, it is (like 6.30) a demand for an authenticating sign – i.e., one that will persuade them to believe in him.
39. Some commentators have followed Bultmann's suggestion that John made use of a 'signs source'. See, in particular, Robert T. Fortna, *The Gospel of Signs*; for a very recent discussion see John Ashton, *Studying John: Approaches to the Fourth Gospel*, 90–113. Others remain sceptical. Our concern, however, is with the way John has handled the tradition, and not with theories of its origin.
40. There are signs of this kind of blurring in 11.27, where Martha states that she believes Jesus to be 'the Messiah, the Son of God,

the one coming into the world'.

41. John 20.30f.
42. We conclude that the Fourth Evangelist reserved the term *sēmeia* for the actions of Jesus, and did not regard the Baptist as having performed a sign. See Chapter I, n.62.
43. This is true of every occasion on which the noun *ergon* is attributed to Jesus. In the case of 7.21, the apparent exception to this rule, it is clear from the context (vv.16–18, 28f.) that Jesus' 'one work' is the work of God. In 6.28f., the work of God required from those who hear Jesus is that they should believe in him. The other references are: 4.34; 5.20, 36; 9.3f.; 10.25, 32, 37f.; 14.10–12; 15.24; 17.4.
44. John 9.16, 29–33.
45. John 9.38.
46. John 9.3.
47. John 7.30; 8.20; 12.23, 27; 13.1; 17.1.
48. Matt.26.61//Mark14.58. Luke does not have this saying.
49. John 3.14–21; 4.13–15, 25f., 29, 39–42.
50. John 3.14–18.
51. Num. 21.8f. The LXX uses the phrase *epi sēmeiou* here to translate the Hebrew *'al nēs*, 'on a high pole'. Was it this that attracted the evangelist's attention to the passage?
52. This is surely the correct meaning of the Greek here. It is the interpretation given to the verse by many of the Fathers, though an alternative reading, followed by many commentators (and going back to Origen), interprets the *autou* in v.38 as referring to the believer, not Jesus: the *NRSV* even inserts the words 'the believer's' into the text! For a discussion of the probabilities, see R. E. Brown, *The Gospel according to John I–XII*, 320f. If my interpretation of the context of the saying is correct, it *must* have been intended as a reference to Jesus as the source of the waters.
53. Ex. 17.1–7; Num. 20.2–13.
54. John 7.39 points us forward to the time of Jesus' glorification.
55. John 12.1–8.
56. Luke 7.36–50.
57. Cf. R. E. Brown, *The Gospel according to John I–XII*, 454.
58. John 10.16.
59. John 5.25–29; 11.25f.
60. John 3.14; 8.28; 12.32–34.
61. John 12.23; 13.31.

62. John 18.33–40; 19.8–16.
63. John 19.1–5, 17–22.
64. John 13.1–20.
65. Cf. Matt. 10.24, 40; 18.1–5; 20.24–28; Mark 9.33–37; 10.41–45; Luke 6.40; 9.48; 22.24–27.
66. Matt. 26.21–25//Mark 14.18,21. Cf. Luke 22.21–23.
67. John 13.21–30.
68. John 21.1–14.
69. J. Duncan M. Derrett, 'Law in the New Testament: The Story of the Woman Taken in Adultery'.
70. R. E. Brown, *The Gospel according to John I–XII*, 334.
71. J. Jeremias, *The Parables of Jesus*, 228.
72. R. Schnackenburg, *The Gospel according to St John*, Vol.2, 166.
73. T. W. Manson, 'The Pericope de Adultera (Joh 7^{53}—8^{11})'.
74. Ambrose, *Ep.* 26 (*PL* 16, col.1089); Augustine, *Contra adversarium legis et prophetarum* I (*PL* 42, col. 630–1); Jerome, *Dial. contra Pelagianos* II (*PL* 23, col. 553). This view is also supported by Jeremias, *Parables* (n. 71) and Schnackenburg, *Gospel* (n. 72).
75. The *NRSV* here follows Dahood's suggestion that the Hebrew *'eretz* refers to the underworld; see 'The Value of Ugaritic for Textual Criticism', 164–8. The traditional translation given above (which is supported by the LXX) seems far more likely. The actual meaning of the two interpretations is very similar, but the reference to 'dust' or 'ground' is necessary to make the passage relevant to the incident in the Fourth Gospel.
76. The passage is missing from many early mss, and its style and vocabulary are not typical of John. One ms places the passage after 7.36, some Georgian mss after 7.44, thus linking the story even more closely with the teaching in 7.37–44. Others place it at the end of the Gospel.
77. Matt. 11.9//Luke 7.26.
78. In John 20.30f., we are told that the author has written about the signs *hina pisteu[s]ete hoti Iēsous estin ho Christos ho Huios tou Theou,* the *s* in square brackets indicating a reading which gives a different tense. If we adopt the present tense, the readers of the gospel are presumably already Christians; if the aorist tense is correct, then they *could* be (but are not necessarily) non-Christians. In view of what John says about signs elsewhere, it is more likely that his purpose should be understood to be to confirm and develop faith, rather than to create it in those who do

not yet believe.
79. See Chapter I, 4f.
80. Mark 1.27.

Appendix: The Lord's Supper as Prophetic Drama

1. David Daube, *He that Cometh*; 'The Significance of the Afiko-man', 4f.; *Wine in the Bible*; Deborah Bleicher Carmichael, 'David Daube on the Eucharist and the Passover Seder'.
2. *Prophetic Drama in the Old Testament*.

Index of References

THE BIBLE

OTHER JEWISH WRITINGS

OTHER CHRISTIAN WRITINGS

Index of Modern Authors